Books in the FT Press Project Management Series

Mastering Project, Program, and Portfolio Management: Models for Structuring and Executing the Project Hierarchy

Lister (ISBN: 0133839745)

Mastering Principles and Practices in PMBOK, Prince 2, and Scrum

Roudias (ISBN: 0134060814)

Mastering Project Human Resource Management: Effectively Organize and Communicate with All Project Stakeholders

Singh (ISBN: 0133837890)

Mastering Project Management Integration and Scope: A Framework for Strategizing and Defining Project Objectives and Deliverables

Sokowski (ISBN: 0133886425)

A Comprehensive Guide to Project Management Schedule and Cost Control: Methods and Models for Managing the Project Lifecycle

Wilson (ISBN: 0133573117)

Mastering Risk and Procurement in Project Management: A Guide to Planning, Controlling, and Resolving Unexpected Problems

Wilson (ISBN: 0133837904)

Mastering Project Time Management, Cost Control, and Quality Management

Wilson (ISBN: 0133839753)

Mastering Project Management Strategy and Processes: Proven Methods to Meet Organizational Goals

Wilson (ISBN: 0133854167)

Mastering Project Management Strategy and Processes

Mastering Project Management Strategy and Processes

Proven Methods to Meet Organizational Goals

Randal Wilson

Publisher: Paul Boger
Editor in Chief: Amy Neidlinger
Executive Editor: Jeanne Glasser Levine
Operations Specialist: Jodi Kemper
Cover Designer: Chuti Prasertsith
Managing Editor: Kristy Hart
Project Editor: Elaine Wiley
Copy Editor: Cheri Clark
Proofreader: Sarah Kearns
Senior Indexer: Cheryl Lenser
Compositor: Nonie Ratcliff
Manufacturing Buyer: Dan Uhrig

© 2015 by Randal Wilson
Upper Saddle River, New Jersey 07458

For information about buying this title in bulk quantities, or for special sales opportunities (which may include electronic versions; custom cover designs; and content particular to your business, training goals, marketing focus, or branding interests), please contact our corporate sales department at corpsales@pearsoned.com or (800) 382-3419.

For government sales inquiries, please contact governmentsales@pearsoned.com.

For questions about sales outside the U.S., please contact international@pearsoned.com.

Company and product names mentioned herein are the trademarks or registered trademarks of their respective owners.

Printed in the United States of America
First Printing January 2015

ISBN-10: 0-13-385416-7
ISBN-13: 978-0-13-385416-9

Pearson Education LTD.
Pearson Education Australia PTY, Limited
Pearson Education Singapore, Pte. Ltd.
Pearson Education Asia, Ltd.
Pearson Education Canada, Ltd.
Pearson Educación de Mexico, S.A. de C.V.
Pearson Education—Japan
Pearson Education Malaysia, Pte. Ltd.

Library of Congress Control Number: 2014954707

I would like to dedicate this book to my wife, Dusty, and sons, Nolan, Garrett, and Carlin, for their support and patience through this project.

Contents

About the Author

Randal Wilson, MBA, PMP, serves as Visiting Professor of Project Management, Keller Graduate School of Management, at the Elk Grove, California, DeVry University campus. His teaching style is one of addressing project management concepts using not only academic course guidelines and text, but also in-depth discussions in lectures using practical application from industry experience.

Mr. Wilson is currently Operations and Project Manager at Parker Hose and Fittings. He is responsible for five locations across Northern California and Nevada, as well as project management of redesigns and renovation of existing facilities and construction of new facilities.

Mr. Wilson was formerly in the telecommunications industry as Senior New Product Introduction Engineer at REMEC, Inc.; Senior New Product Introduction Engineer with Spectrian Corp.; and Associate Design Engineer with American Microwave Technology. He also served as Senior Manufacturing Engineer at Hewlett-Packard.

He is a certified Project Management Professional (PMP) of the Project Management Institute. He acquired an MBA with concentration in General Operations Management from Keller Graduate School of Management of DeVry University in Fremont, California, and a Bachelor of Science in Technical Management with concentration in Project Management from DeVry University in Fremont, California.

Introduction

Throughout time, man has understood the basic concept of efficiency as the amount of work required to generate a desired benefit from the work. This concept can take us back to the time when man had to invest a given amount of work in preparing and maintaining a field of crops versus the benefit of the crops that were harvested. Because the field of crops would typically yield the same amount of harvest each year, man devised ways to prepare, maintain, and harvest the crops faster each year, improving his efficiency in the work required to produce the harvest. We use the same philosophy in organizations today, called process development and process improvement.

Successful organizations improve their efficiency, generally measured in bottom-line profits, through the use of process development and process improvement. Processes are typically a selection of activities grouped with a specific objective, making it easier to manage and control completion of the process objective. The critical element found in most effective processes is not only in the grouping of specific activities, but more in the organization of activities. Organizations might be very good at developing work activities to accomplish organizational objectives and may even group activities in the form of departments or divisions within an organization. When organizations take the added step of forming a process using grouped work activities, these activities can be organized in logical and sequential order such that they can be quantified as to their importance, prioritization, cost structure, and estimated time duration requirements and such that focus on organizing activities makes the process efficient. As we will see in this book, processes can be used strategically as well as tactically to accomplish objectives at several levels within the organization.

How Projects Are Used to Accomplish Objectives

As organizations develop processes to accomplish objectives, these processes can be the organization of activities carried out on a daily basis or can be activities carried out to accomplish a one-time and unique objective that we call a *project*. Organizations that are split up into departments, such as accounting, human resources, engineering, manufacturing and process engineering, warehouse, and shipping and receiving, have processes that document specific activities that are carried out on a daily basis. These activities typically are not unique, but are what is required of that department on an ongoing basis.

When a department has to engage in a process development exercise, process improvement, or a documentation development exercise, these are unique and not typical of day-to-day operations, and the activities required can be grouped into a project. Some organizations that have unique output deliverables as their day-to-day operations, such as construction companies producing unique building structures, can actually organize work activities into projects for these primary organizational objectives. Grouping activities into projects can be done at several levels within the organization to accomplish higher, more strategic-level objectives in which executives are trying to accomplish major objectives, as well as lower-level or tactical objectives.

Strategic and Tactical Use of Projects

As organizations begin to understand the value of using projects in day-to-day operations, this organizational tool can be used at a tactical level in the production of goods and services, as well as a higher strategic level by executives. Owners, board of directors members, and executives within the organization sometimes have major objectives that have to be accomplished, and the organization of work activities in the form of a project is extremely useful to ensure that everything has been completed correctly. Projects can be used to evaluate future market strategies, growth opportunities, the expansion and creation of new facilities, and strategic funding or financing opportunities.

Organizations that use projects at a tactical level discover that projects are useful in process development or improvement, documentation development, new product development, or any other unique endeavor conducted within a department. In many cases, projects are used more at the tactical level to accomplish specific and unique goals or objectives throughout an operation. Projects can be used to accomplish very small and insignificant objectives, as well as larger, more complex objectives required within an operation. The important aspect of using projects is the fact that they can be used to organize all the activities required to produce a unique objective that is not associated with daily activities. If an organization is structured such that projects are used on a regular basis, this can constitute the development of a project management structure that can further organize projects depending on the requirements of the operation.

Project Structures

An organization that is using projects on a regular basis falls under one of two categories: *projectized* organizational structure or *matrix* organizational structure. Projectized organizations have unique deliverables as a normal part of daily operations and therefore require projects to manage the development of these deliverables. The efficiency of the organization is in the management of all the activities required to produce these unique deliverables, and project managers are hired to design a project as well as manage the project to closure. Matrix organizations are similar to functional organizations that simply utilize projects as a regular part of their day-to-day operations. This is typically in the form of new product development, process development and improvement exercises conducted, and engineering and manufacturing environments.

In the projectized and matrix organizational structures when projects are used on a regular basis, the need for further organization might require grouping of similar projects into what is called a *program*. If an organization has a requirement by a specific customer for several different project output deliverables, each of these projects can be grouped into one single program designated for a specific customer. In other cases, the organization might have several products that fall within a similar category and might want to group projects into a program based on product type. Organizations typically hire a program manager to oversee like projects within a program to ensure that the program directive is being carried out.

If an organization grows in size such that there might be several programs operating, as well as many projects, the organization might group programs and projects into larger categories called portfolios. Organizations typically hire a manager to oversee a portfolio because the portfolio is a large component of programs and projects specific to a particular customer, product type, or market. This is another way to strategically group projects and programs to accomplish organizational objectives. Organizations can divide the operations into large divisions called portfolios that focus on specific elements within the organization. The focus within the organization of grouping work activities into projects, grouping like projects into programs, and grouping various programs and projects into large portfolios is all part of an efficiency exercise in the strategic use of project management.

Projects as Groups of Processes

When we look at specific aspects of what makes a project efficient, it is typically the organization of activities into processes and the alignment of processes that form a project. When an organization at a tactical level has a directive to accomplish a specific objective, organizing work activities in the form of a project can sometimes produce various project structures. It is the specific organization of various processes that determines what type of project structure might be used to accomplish a particular objective. Some objectives might be straightforward, such as the development of a particular product that can be broken down into several smaller pieces, and might be well-defined as to the development of what activities are required to complete the objective. In other cases, an objective might be more elusive and cannot be well defined as to the specific steps required to accomplish the objective, requiring a different type of project structure.

This text introduces six models of project structure that can accommodate various types of project objectives. If the breakdown of work activities for a specific project can be well defined, this can be one type of project structure. Other objectives might have a well-defined final output objective, but these objectives cannot be broken down into subcomponents that can be well defined and therefore require a different project structure that can accommodate incremental or repetitive cycles of development. This text goes into the details of how various project structures can be developed to accommodate many types of project objectives.

Project Process Interactions

When processes have been developed and organized within a project structure, these processes might not always be independent of each other or other elements of daily operations within an organization. The Project Management Institute, in its publication of *Project Management Body of Knowledge (PMBOK), Fifth Edition*, lists specific processes that project managers can use in managing project work activities to completion. In many cases, we find that there are interactions between processes that need to be managed at the project level, as well as these processes interacting with operations within the organization. Process interactions can be in several different forms, and in this book we cover various forms of how processes can interact with each other and what effects these processes can have on an organization at the tactical level.

Process interactions can be in several different forms in which the basic project management processes, such as the initiating, planning, executing, monitoring, and controlling, as well as closing, can interact with each other during the course of conducting project activities. For example, processes associated with monitoring and controlling can affect the executing process. Items associated with the initiating process can affect planning. In some cases, items associated with the execution process can have drastic effects on the closing process. This book covers several interactions between these different project management processes, as well as the influence of knowledge areas within each process. The Project Management Institute, in *PMBOK*,

Fifth Edition, has also outlined knowledge areas that represent the responsibilities of a project manager for tasks carried out throughout the project life cycle. It is interesting to contrast how these knowledge areas correspond to and interact with the five process groups. In some cases, interactions of certain knowledge areas with other knowledge areas can actually produce what are called *compound interactions*. This book goes into the details of how project managers can use certain knowledge areas to influence other knowledge areas, creating these compound interactions. As project managers come to understand the use of project management process groups and how knowledge areas can be used to manage various aspects of project activities, this gives the project managers tools and techniques to effectively and efficiently manage projects to completion.

Why Organizations Benefit from Projects

As organizations utilize projects more and more to effectively manage the completion of both strategic and tactical objectives, it will become evident that it is the structure of projects based on the organization of activities and the systematic use of specific project management processes that make the use of projects within an organization a powerful tool. It is important for organizations to understand that although processes, by definition of the use of organizational tools and techniques, can be a formidable asset in accomplishing the strategic and tactical objectives, it is the use of project managers skilled, educated, and experienced in project management who will carry out these processes to benefit the organization. Project managers typically stand apart from functional managers and executive managers because they have experience in project management tools and techniques, as well as the practical application of processes and process interactions that make projects a powerful tool within an organization. When organizations grow and become successful, that success is generally from the reality of understanding the value of process development, which may include the use of projects to manage accomplishing both strategic and tactical objectives. Organizations are better and more efficient at conducting daily operations in accomplishing strategic objectives through the use of project processes.

1

Project Structure

1.1 Introduction

In today's increasingly complex world of corporate strategies attempting to respond to various market demands, projects are a primary tool used regularly to accomplish business strategic objectives. Projects, although having differing levels of complexity, can fundamentally be broken down into a rather simplistic organized structure of activities, processes, and natural phases of development that can be easily understood as viewed from a high level. We use the term *high level* to establish the vantage point from which this chapter will address the general nature of a project and characterize the development of a project from start to finish.

Although projects can vary in size and complexity, as well as in the structure of activities based on the type of deliverable the project is required to produce, projects will have two primary components that define *how* the project will be carried out: *stages of progression* and *project processes*. It's important for project managers and students of project management to understand the difference between the stages of progression, sometimes referred to as phases, and the processes required throughout the project to complete work activities. The stages of progression, as viewed at a high level, are common across most projects and represent the basic elements of development through the life of a project called the *Project Life Cycle*.

This chapter covers the general stages of progression through a project, the organizational and project-level elements that can influence each stage, and the general character of the life cycle that would suggest a specific project structure based on the type of project output deliverable. It is important to understand a clear separation between the stages of development through a project life cycle and the project processes that would be carried out during the project life cycle; this mislabeling is a common occurrence with project managers and individuals studying project management when they confuse project processes as being the stages in the project life cycle. This chapter focuses on the stages of progression through the project life cycle, and project processes are covered in detail in Chapter 4, "Project Management Processes." The scope of this chapter is at a higher, broader perspective of the entire project to allow the conceptual understanding of the project life cycle.

1.2 Project Life Cycle

As we look at the characteristics of projects, at a high level, projects tend to take on a common theme of stages as the project develops and progresses from beginning to end. The project manager understanding these fundamental stages at the beginning of a project can separate general areas of the project life to better categorize what has to be completed during each stage. This will help the project manager focus on more specific tasks and processes that will need to be completed at each stage. This concept will be similar in thought process to the project manager evaluating a proposed project deliverable, at the beginning of a project, as a single component, and automatically visualizing the component broken down into subcomponents and those subcomponents into smaller components to understand what each of the smallest level work activities will need to be. Viewing the overall project as a single entity and seeing the project broken up into major components, those components broken down into smaller processes, and those processes broken down into actual activities, will help the project manager understand his role in not only managing the smaller project work activities, but also keeping an eye on what has been completed throughout the project and what lies ahead.

What Is a Project?

Let's start off by recapping the fundamental definition of a project to clarify the difference between a project and a component of normal daily business operations. Organizations can be structured to carry out many types of operations that might include the following:

- Manufacturing environments are producing products on a repetitive and ongoing basis.
- Engineering departments are conducting research and development on prototype product for a customer.
- Accounting departments are performing daily accounting operations.
- Sales and marketing are performing regular defined tasks to advance awareness of an organization's business and generate sales.
- Shipping and receiving departments are regularly packaging and shipping items, as well as receiving items that are being delivered to the facility.
- Software companies are creating general software packages and specialized packages and enhancements for specific customers.
- Law offices are reviewing and producing legal documents, as well as providing legal representation.
- Construction companies are building and creating unique facilities and structures within our society.

With each type of business operation listed, we can see examples of work activities that are performed on a daily basis, as well as items that might be unique to a specific customer need. Organizations that design, develop, and manufacture products will find themselves in a position to have the opportunity to both create a one-time unique item for a specific customer, and then produce an item repetitively on an ongoing basis. Other organizations might provide a service, such as a law firm that can either produce a one-time unique legal service or provide ongoing legal service of similar activity for an organization or individual. In the case of a construction company, they produce a unique structure for a specific customer but do this as the primary component of their strategic business objective. In all of these cases, organizations will be in a position either to have a repetitive ongoing activity or to create or provide a unique one-time service or deliverable.

When organizations have an operation that performs a service or produces a deliverable on an ongoing basis, that service or deliverable, although having a start, does not necessarily have an end, and the same activity will be carried out until it is no longer necessary. Projects, on the other hand, will have a definite start but will also "produce a unique one-time service or deliverable" and will stop when that objective has been completed. The Project Management Institute (PMI) defines a project in their publication, *A Guide to the Project Management Body of Knowledge (PMBOK®), Fifth Edition*, this way:

> "A *temporary endeavor undertaken to create a unique product, service, or result.*"

As we can see by this definition, projects are characterized as being "unique" and "temporary" and therefore can be separated from the daily operations that organizations carry out on a repetitive and ongoing basis.

In looking back at our list of organizations and corresponding operations (given previously), we can clearly see now that some organizations perform regular, repetitive, and ongoing tasks such as manufacturing, accounting, sales and marketing, shipping and receiving, and providing regular services. In other cases, an organization might produce a unique item or service one time for a specific customer that can be considered "a project," such as engineering developing a prototype, development of a specific software package or enhancement for a customer, a law office providing a one-time legal representation, or a construction company building a unique structure. It is important to understand the difference between normal daily *ongoing* operation activities and *one-time unique endeavors* in which projects have a defined beginning, a period of planning, a course of work to be carried out, and a defined end at which point the project deliverable or service is finally accepted by the customer.

Project Stages of Progression (Life Cycle)

Now that we understand that a project has a defined beginning, work needs to be completed, and there is a defined ending point, we can study the characteristics of each stage a project goes through in the course of a project life cycle. The natural progression or "nature" of a project goes through four primary stages: *conceptual and approval, planning, execution,* and *closure.* All projects large or small, simple or complex, pass through all four of these stages because each stage is required in effectively carrying out and completing a project. These stages, within the project life cycle, should be viewed as the natural progression or development of a project understood as the logical succession of development any project would need to go through for completion.

This logical progression of an endeavor is the case with business or in our personal life in completing an endeavor. We start the endeavor with evaluating the necessity and approving the idea of moving forward, plan activities that we want to carry out, conduct the activities, and evaluate the final result, and, when satisfied, determine that the endeavor has been completed. Because these four stages of progression are typical for most things that we would set out to complete, it is easy and logical to associate these stages with all projects that will be conducted. Figure 1.1 graphically depicts the four stages of development and progression that projects will pass through generally associated with producing a project objective (deliverable), as well as the workload associated with each stage.

Project Concept and Approval

Because a project is a unique endeavor, and is not something associated with normal daily operations, it is an endeavor that has been created out of a unique necessity (can be either external or internal to the organization) and therefore has an originator (customer) who has a specific goal in mind. The beginning of this endeavor then starts with the creation of a unique goal and is defined as the *deliverable.*

Projects can be internal to an organization, in which one department wants to develop something usually associated with process improvement and creates a project based on a unique endeavor to address a specific area of improvement. That department or functional manager then defines the goal or deliverable intended and outlines specifics as to what will be required to satisfy the conditions of that goal. In another case, an external customer might have a unique requirement for the organization and submit specifications or a statement of work (SOW) outlining what is required. In either case, when a project begins, a customer has a defined goal (deliverable), and the organization needs to conduct an evaluation to ascertain the feasibility of completing the intended goal and, based on the outcome of this evaluation, authorize the endeavor, approving the creation of a project—and this forms the first stage of the project called the *concept and approval stage*.

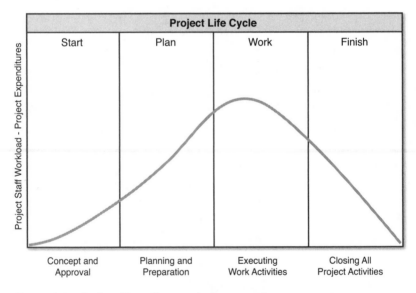

Figure 1.1   Project life cycle stages of progression.

During the concept and approval stage, individuals within the organization identified with the responsibility to evaluate and approve projects for the organization (which might or might not include the project manager) spend time communicating with the customer (internal or external) to evaluate information to better understand the endeavor. The goal of these initial meetings with the customer is to provide enough information to determine whether the project is a good fit for the organization and its own business strategic objective, if it is feasible, and whether it benefits the organization strategically, financially, or operationally. Chapter 4 outlines the specific project processes that are carried out and output deliverables required during this phase of the project life cycle.

Project Planning and Preparation

After the endeavor has been approved and authorized, it is then called a project and resources can be assigned to the project to begin the *planning and preparation stage*. During the conceptual time of the project, depending on how the organization is structured and the processes to assign project managers to potential projects, project managers might be involved in the concept and approval stage, but if not, they will be assigned at the beginning of the planning and preparation stage. It is important for the project manager to understand the outcome of communications with the customer regarding the project deliverable and overall project goal. This will form the basic understanding of what the project manager will be managing and how she is to proceed in developing a project plan.

As shown in Figure 1.1, the planning and preparation stage has more activity and staff associated with the project than at the first stage, because more work is required during this stage. During the planning and preparation stage, the project manager reviews all the project management processes that will be carried and assesses what staff will be required in assisting in the planning and preparation process. The project manager also spends a significant amount of time reviewing communications with the customer, specifications, statement of work, and any other details regarding the project deliverable to formulate an understanding of the project objective. The time spent in the planning and preparation stage of a project can vary greatly depending on the size and complexity of the project objective and how many resources are required to complete all the processes during this stage. This stage is one of the most important stages because it is where the project manager outlines several specific processes and develops various plans such as budget and schedule development, resource management, risk management, stakeholder management, procurement management, and quality management. The project manager must allocate enough time at the beginning of the project to effectively complete all the actions required during the planning phase before work can actually begin to ensure that the project has been designed properly and all required management tools have been developed. Chapter 4 outlines all the specific processes required during the planning stage, as well as any output deliverables that need to be produced by the project manager.

Project Execution

Now that the project manager has successfully planned the project work activities and has developed all project management plans that will be required, it is time to begin work on activities required to complete the project deliverable. This is called the *execution stage*. As shown in Figure 1.1, the execution stage of the project results in most of the work, resources, and finances expended in carrying out project work activities. The project manager's role during the execution stage shifts from planning to an activity manager role, and this requires monitoring and controlling work activities to maintain the project budget, schedule, and quality of the deliverable. Because risk events are typically more associated with work activities, more risk events are likely to occur during this phase, and the project manager needs to manage risk responses to maintain the budget, schedule, and quality of the deliverable. Chapter 4 outlines all the specific processes required during the execution phase. Chapter 6, "Project Process Interactions," outlines various interactions of project processes and project management knowledge areas during this phase. The primary output of the execution stage is the acceptance of the main project deliverable required by the customer.

Project Closure

The last stage in the project life cycle begins when the customer officially accepts the project deliverable as having met all expectations and an initiative can be set by the project manager to begin closing out all activities associated with the project, called the *closure stage*.

As shown in Figure 1.1, the closing stage of a project has a significant reduction of all resources, financial expenditures, and any supporting activities required throughout the organization specific to the project. This final stage of the project can be difficult and is probably the least understood of all four stages by most project managers, who might underestimate what has to be completed to officially close a project. It is common for project managers and most project staff, as well as executives within the organization, to consider a project finished when a customer has accepted a project deliverable. At this point, the project manager is usually assigned to another project and the focus easily moves on to the next tasks that need to be completed for the new project, rather than ensuring that all the things that need to be officially completed on the prior project have been addressed.

For example, closing project activities can be likened to starting a project in the garage in which you take out lots of tools, supplies, and materials you'll need in order to create something, thus making a general mess of the garage. After the item has been created, everybody takes off to the next activity, leaving the garage a mess. Obviously, although the deliverable was created, the project is far from over because the garage needs to be cleaned and everything needs to be put away. This is also like creating a large dinner for family members and having the kitchen cluttered with pots and pans and food items, leaving the kitchen in a general mess. Although the dinner was a great success, accepted thankfully and wonderfully enjoyed by all family members, the project is far from over because the kitchen needs to be cleaned and everything should be put away.

Project managers have lots of responsibilities throughout the project life cycle, and although most of them have to do with planning and executing work activities to successfully produce a project deliverable, project managers have a large responsibility to ensure that all project activities, contractual commitments, and procurements are successfully completed and closed out. The project manager should always view the end of a project with this thought:

"Is the customer happy with the deliverable and have I put away everything from the project?"

Although this can be a trivial question, it's an extremely important one because the project manager is responsible for ensuring that the customer has accepted the deliverable and that everything associated with the project has been completely closed.

The first primary area of importance with project closure is ensuring that the customer not only has received the deliverable, but also has formally approved its acceptance. There have been cases in which project managers have provided a deliverable, assuming that the customer was happy, and dismissed all project staff and closed activities, only to find out that the customer had remaining issues that did not get addressed, which created larger problems for the organization. The project manager has the ultimate responsibility to ensure that the customer is completely satisfied and has officially signed off acceptance of a project deliverable.

The second primary area of importance, after the customer has signed off acceptance of the output deliverable, involves terminating things have been put in place during the course of the project to avoid financial or legal problems. For all contracts used throughout the project, it needs to be verified that they have run their course and all conditions have been met. In many cases, contracts will have a closeout instruction that indicates what conditions have to be met in order for the contract to be determined fulfilled. If these conditions are not met, legal actions can be taken against the organization that can have severe financial ramifications. In many cases, procurements throughout the project might have resulted in purchases having to be returned with new items sent, and these purchase transactions can remain open for several months after a project has closed, not being addressed. If projects have used facilities, equipment, and materials within the organization, the project manager is responsible to ensure that things have been returned and facilities have been put back in proper order before the project can be considered closed. Chapter 4 outlines any specific processes required during the closure stage of the project life cycle.

As we have seen, all projects in general will pass through each of these four stages of the project life cycle in fundamental development and progression. The project manager should take each stage as a separate component of the project and focus on the processes within each stage to ensure that everything that is normally conducted in each stage has been successfully completed. Depending on the size and complexity of a project, some projects that have extremely long durations might experience a reoccurrence of the planning stage within the execution stage where segments of the project deliverable were not completely defined during the conceptual stage. The important aspect of understanding the project life cycle is to know that all projects will have a conceptual and approval component, a planning component, and an execution of work activities component, as well as a requirement for project closure.

1.3 Project Life Cycle Influences

As project managers design and manage projects, they will likely run into problems and roadblocks that might alter what happens to a project during the project life cycle. Project managers know and understand that problems are inevitable, and they typically plan responses to problems (risks responses) during the planning stage of the life cycle designed to mitigate or eliminate the effects the risk might have on the project. Risks are defined as problems that can be identified in advance of the project, and responses can be developed in case those problems occur. Uncertainties, however, are also problems, but problems that cannot be planned for because they are unknown or unexpected at the beginning of a project and therefore present real issues for the project manager. These can be "acts of God" with regard to weather or earthquakes, or they can be the effects of change with regard to business conditions or management decisions that could not have been planned for at the beginning of a project.

Regardless of how these uncertainties arise, they can influence the project and how a project moves through the project life cycle. We look at life cycle influences at two primary levels: the *strategic level*, having to do primarily with a higher level generally associated with the organization and business environment, and the *tactical level*, relating to lower-level items specific to project work activities. Each of these two levels can involve things that can significantly influence projects as they move through the project life cycle, requiring a project to move from one stage in the life cycle immediately to another stage and requiring the project manager to respond accordingly. One example would be a business condition in which a customer has a significant change request while the project is in the execution stage, requiring the project to move back to the planning stage. Another example would be management making a decision to terminate a project prematurely, requiring the project to move from a planning or execution stage directly to closure. Regardless of what the condition is, the project manager should be aware of conditions that can influence a project and what affects that would have on the project life cycle.

Organizational (Strategic Level)

Organizations are constantly under pressure to evaluate their success based on their general business strategy, which can include what products or services they are offering and their general position in the marketplace. This might require executives within the organization to make adjustments periodically to realign the business strategy with a successful road map positioning them better in the marketplace. These adjustments typically require changes within the organization, and how these changes are managed can affect projects within the organization.

Some effects of change might require projects to be simply terminated because they no longer fall within the business strategy. Projects internal to the organization might have changes that shift the project from an execution stage back to a planning stage to alter a project deliverable slightly. Customers that have the organization creating a unique product for them might have a business condition requiring them to make significant changes on the product, which requires the product to move from an execution or planning stage back to a planning or conceptual stage based on new specifications. These types of changes can affect a project and where the project falls within the life cycle. When changes occur, it's important for the project manager to understand the conditions the changes might be derived from and the big picture of how the changes affect not only the project life cycle, but other areas within the organization.

- **Business conditions**—One of the typical areas that can influence the project within the project life cycle involves issues stemming from business conditions that are simply higher-level decisions, conditions, or outcomes of what the operation has to contend with in the course of conducting business. Some of these conditions might include the following:

- *Competition*—When projects internal to the organization are conducted for the purpose of developing and engineering a prototype, sales and marketing typically have a close eye focused on competition, and changes to the prototype might be required that will shift the project from one stage in the life cycle to another. In some cases, it is simply altering some component of the product such that it will compete better within the marketplace (the project moves from execution back to planning). In other cases, it might be terminating a product altogether (the project moves from planning or execution directly to closure) because engineering has missed the time-to-market window and engineering resources would be better spent on a new product. Issues stemming from situations in the competition are higher-level business decisions and do not reflect problems at the project or tactical level—the project manager has done nothing wrong, but rather this is simply a high-level business decision.

- *High-level customer issues*—This is similar to the competition issue in that this is out of the hands of the project manager and is not at the project or tactical level, but it is at a higher level regarding customer issues with the organization. In some cases, customers might have credit issues and are not able to pay for a project deliverable, and as a result a project has been terminated (the project moves from planning or execution directly to closure). Customers might find that they lack the technical abilities to correctly articulate project specifications and/or are blaming the organization for misinterpreting specifications or the statement of work requesting that a project deliverable be continually updated (the project has to move back and forth between execution and planning). The customer representative might have had a falling out with an individual or a department within the organization and the customer wants to terminate a project (the project moves from conceptual, planning, or execution directly to closure). It is always a risk when an organization engages in business with the customer external to the organization because there might be times when uncertainties regarding the relationship turn sour, forcing unfortunate business decisions.

- *Time-to-market issues*—When projects internal to the organization that will be designed as a prototype for future production are in the conceptual stage, marketing and sales generally have input as to the relevance of a particular endeavor with regard to timing and when the deliverable would be available for sale. This is called time-to-market. During the conceptual phase, a general assessment is usually made as to the time frame required for a project, and this is important to ensure that the output deliverable will be ready for a specific market or customer. Because these projects are typically prototypes, it is all the more important to get these initial products into the hands of specific customers to lock in production commitments. If sales and marketing do not believe that a prototype can be finished by a specific time, there is a risk that the customer might simply acquire the item from a competitor and the organization will lose out on a critical opportunity. This will be doubly important because not only would the organization have lost out on a product opportunity, but they would have expended project resources in the course of development that could have been used elsewhere. This decision would be to terminate a project and does not reflect on the project manager's ability, but simply is a marketing decision to utilize project resources elsewhere (moves a project from conceptual or planning to closure).

- **Management**—Organizations with management structures might have different ways management and executives interact with project activities, which can influence decisions made regarding projects. Managers, informing project managers of a decision that will affect the project, might simply be acting in response to an overall business decision that was made by a collective body of management or executives. In other cases, individuals within the management structure might direct project managers, regarding their project, in such a way that they influence a project within the life cycle solely out of issues with that individual manager. Although this is unfortunate, this can be a condition within the organization that the project manager will have to deal with and can result in an action needing to be carried out that will have an unfortunate impact on a project.

- *Lack of upper management support*—Depending on the type of organization, the size and complexity of a project, and the type of project, project managers might find certain individuals within the upper management structure that simply do not support the project and will make managing project activities difficult. In many cases, project managers have to work with other functional managers on resource allocations, and if those managers do not view the project as important, they will make acquiring resources for project activities difficult (the project is stuck in the planning or execution stage for extended periods). Upper or executive management might not all agree on the project during the conceptual stage, creating problems for the project manager in getting approval for a project to move out of the conceptual stage to the planning stage. If executives have veto power, this could even require the project to move from a planning stage back to a conceptual stage or to a closure stage.

- *Managerial conflicting agendas*—Managers or upper management might be in agreement with the general idea of a project, but might have a conflicting agenda as to how the project is run or what the project objective is supposed to be. This is usually the case with projects internal to an organization that are intended for one department under the direction of a particular functional manager, when another functional manager or executive wants to influence the project deliverable to benefit himself. Although this can be unfortunate, it is not uncommon for functional managers to disagree on the purpose of a project or specifics regarding a project deliverable (projects can move back and forth between planning and execution stages).

- *Poor communication within management structure*—As much as organizations would like to boast that they have stellar communication among their management staff, this is generally not the case and projects can suffer as a result. For projects, this can be poor communication, internal to an organization, during the conceptual stage regarding the statement of work for a potential project, among managers assigned planning activities and among managers assigned the oversight of project work activities during the execution stage. This type of miscommunication can result in various effects on project work activities, project management processes, and the success or failure of progress through the project life cycle (projects stuck in one stage or moving back and forth between stages).

- *Lack of experienced management*—Organizations that typically do not conduct projects very often will not generally staff their management with individuals experienced in project management processes, and this can create problems for project managers. If the project manager reports to an upper-level or executive manager who is inexperienced in project management, the details of each stage of the project life cycle and the project management processes required during each stage will be difficult for an experienced management to understand and might present problems in the oversight of the project manager. This is not the project manager's fault, just simply unfortunate if the project manager has an inexperienced upper management staff that does not understand project management (various problems can result from this situation, including projects moving from stage to stage or premature project termination).

- **Operations**—As we have seen, organizations can be structured to perform projects as their primary business strategy, or can be structured as a traditional functional organization that simply conducts an internal project occasionally. The difference between these two organizations, from a project management standpoint, is that the organization designed for projects will have its operations structured and geared toward the support and operation of projects, reducing the amount of influence the operation can have on a project throughout its life cycle. Organizations that are structured for a business that does not perform projects might be well run and efficient, but will present constraints and challenges to running a project because that is not what they are geared for.

- *Constraints with resource allocation*—The first area that is typically a challenge for projects within an organization is the allocation of resources required throughout the project life cycle. If the organization is not geared toward projects, challenges might be seen during the conceptual and approval stage in just having resources available that are qualified to assess and improve the project. Typically these types of organizations are generally challenged during the planning and execution stage, during which a larger number of human resources are required that might not be available or exist at all within the organization. In some cases, skilled human resources might exist within the organization, but if those people are required on a project, that will take them away from their normal daily activity, reducing the effectiveness of that department.

  With organizations that are geared toward projects, skilled resources are usually associated with the organization, but the challenge is that sharing these resources across projects in the scheduling of resources can present a challenge for the project manager during the conceptual, planning, and execution stages, depending on the type of resource. These types of challenges might not necessarily cause projects to move back and forth within the life cycle, but simply create work shortages and delays within a stage that can affect a project's budget and schedule.

- *Constraints with facility issues*—Constraints with facility, equipment, and material issues are similar to issues in the allocation of resources but might present some added challenges. If, during the planning stage, a project is slated to use a particular facility and that facility is not available when needed, depending on the complexity of the project activity, this might require the project to move from an execution stage back to a planning stage for use of a different facility. If equipment or materials are not available when needed during the execution stage, this might not force the project to move to a different stage, but simply present a delay within that stage, causing the project to be over budget and behind schedule. In some special cases in which a project requires a very specialized facility, a piece of equipment, or material that is no longer available when needed, this can cause the project to move from the planning or execution stage to a closure stage or might necessitate a return to the conceptual stage to revise the project deliverable.

- *Lack of financing*—It is the project manager's hope that during the conceptual and approval stage of the life cycle, a high-level planning budget was developed and approved allowing the project to begin. However, even when financial backing was initially available, financing can always become a problem throughout the project life cycle, depending on business decisions, market conditions, and how the accounting department of an organization is being managed. This type of problem, depending on the size and complexity of a project, can range anywhere from a small critical purchase that was supposed to be made on an individual credit card and reimbursed by the company that could not happen, to an organization losing a line of credit or having to allocate corporate finances elsewhere so as not to fund a project at all. The effect of a financing problem can range from a single work activity in the execution stage being delayed to a project being completely terminated and moving directly to the closure stage. Corporate financing is typically not the responsibility of the project manager but unfortunately, through no fault of the project manager, can present serious or catastrophic issues, and the project can suffer at any point in the project life cycle.

- *Constraints imposed by other departments within the organization*—This is another area where the structure of the organization can play an important role in whether there is experience with projects. Organizations structured to conduct projects as their fundamental business will have departments in support of and focused on the primary objective of ensuring that projects are carried out correctly and efficiently. Although there might be an occasional issue that can influence a component of a project in the life cycle, these are typically small in nature and are easily resolved.

The primary issue with this problem is with organizations that are not structured for projects whose departments are focused on tasks that support their normal daily business operations and will view projects as an additional component of work that they are typically not geared for. Departments such as engineering might find it easy to work with projects because they are used to development and prototyping. Other departments, such as accounting, purchasing, and manufacturing, might find it difficult to support project activities because they normally focus their resources on their daily operations. This can range from the work performed in various departments up through mid-level and upper-level management that can create challenges for projects at any stage within the project life cycle. In some cases, certain functional managers or upper management might require the project manager to perform tasks other than normal due to a lack of management resources.

- **External to the organization**—Another common influence on projects throughout the project life cycle involves issues stemming from areas external to the organization, when the organization itself is not involved with the issue, but rather influences independent of the organization have a severe impact on projects.

  - *Supplier/vendor issues*—One of the most common external influences is the impact that suppliers and vendors, as well as subcontractors, can have throughout the project life cycle. These types of influences typically are seen during the planning and execution stages but can also present challenges during the closing stage if the issues have not been resolved. Examples of problems from suppliers and vendors that would typically be managed through the purchasing department, might include incorrect or damaged items being received from a supplier or vendor that will have to be returned, price changes, and items that are no longer available when needed on the project. Most of these issues are seen during the planning or execution stage and create budget overruns, schedule delays, or reduced quality and materials. If claims or disputes have been issued against the organization by a vendor supplier during the course of the project that have not been resolved, these could be a challenge during the closing stage of the project to ensure that no further actions will be taken by the supplier vendor to resolve the issue. This can result in the closing stage of the project extending for long periods.

- *Legal issues*—As much as an organization would love to have projects run smoothly throughout the project life cycle, there might be times when legal issues can impose serious or catastrophic influences on a project, requiring a project to change stages or moved to the closure stage prematurely. Because projects might require contractual agreements for the use of facilities and equipment, or contractual agreements to obtain specialized human resource subcontractors, contracts are created to protect both parties, and if one party feels there is a breach of contract, legal action might be taken to resolve an issue. Because these types of agreements will typically be negotiated and can commence during the planning and execution stages, serious legal problems can force a project to move from execution back to planning, or from planning back to conceptual, or can force the complete termination of a project, moving it immediately to the closure stage. In most cases, legal action is taken against the organization and will be at the strategic level, but its influence can affect a project at an overall strategic level as well as an individual work activity at the tactical level.

- *Local, state, or federal constraints*—Occasionally, projects require interaction with local, state, or federal agencies, and this can present a challenge for both the organization and the project, depending on what is required by these agencies. In some cases, projects incur special taxation that needs to be addressed by the accounting department within the organization. In some cases, the legal department of an organization might have to review special regulations that the organization has to follow to allow certain project activities. In some cases, certain types of projects from particular types of organizations might have to file formal documents with a government agency as to the creation of a specialized item or specific specialized work activities that require permits or that have to be registered by a particular government agency. These types of constraints might not be constraints at all if the organization is used to these types of projects, whereas organizations that do not typically perform these activities might find working with these types of agencies extremely difficult and cumbersome, resulting in expensive cost overruns and schedule delays. In some cases, agencies might not allow a project to even begin based on the type of work that is being performed. In other cases, a project might be significantly through the execution phase at which point a government agency does not allow a component of work to be performed, causing severe or catastrophic problems for the project and the life cycle.

Project (Tactical Level)

Project managers are primarily responsible for the design and development of a project, as well as managing all the work activities to complete a project deliverable and successfully close a project. As we have seen, project managers have to be mindful of influences on the project throughout the project life cycle from higher organizational-level challenges and constraints that are outside of the project manager's sphere of influence but that the project manager has to deal with. This section deals primarily with influences at the tactical level inside of the scope of the project where the project manager does have control and can make a difference in whether these elements have a mild or severe influence or any influence at all.

- **Management**—With the project manager being the senior official overseeing the project, *management* refers to the project manager and any elements of project management that are within the project manager's control. This includes the background and experience as well as the managing style and leadership of the project manager; the development, mentoring, and management of project teams; and the design, development, and execution of the project plan.

- *Project manager*—If project managers don't know already, the project manager is counted as one of the largest risks a project can have because they are typically responsible for the design, development, and implementation of the entire project plan. Although project managers can be educated, can be trained, and can have experience in project management, they are still human and subject to making mistakes. Because real project managers typically have a higher level of success in managing projects due to their background, it is usually the individual who was selected from within an organization to oversee a project that will have a higher probability of issues and failures throughout the project life cycle.

  Project managers who have an adequate background in project management have developed tools and techniques, over the course of several projects, to manage the design, development, and implementation of all the processes typically required to successfully carry out a project. Project managers understand challenges or issues relative to a breakdown in system or processes and can quickly assess which component of a process has failed and how to resolve the process. Project managers understand the importance of human resource management, risk management, stakeholder management, and procurements management throughout the project life cycle because these are vitally important to project success.

  Individuals who might have management experience overseeing a department, a production line, or some group of staff for processes within the organization do not necessarily know the processes required to successfully design, develop, and implement a project and therefore have a higher probability of failure at various points throughout the project life cycle. This, in most cases, is not necessarily the fault of the manager, who might be a good manager of whatever it is she was managing in the organization; it just points to the fact that the manager is unaware of critical processes required to successfully manage the project. Typical challenges for these types of managers may include the following:

- Inability to break down a project deliverable into its smallest components to understand the details of all work activities required

- Inability to accurately develop a project budget

- Inability to accurately develop a project schedule

- Inability to develop a comprehensive risk management plan

- Inability to effectively manage stakeholder expectations

- Inability to effectively manage procurements

- Inability to effectively manage quality control of the project deliverable

Normal functional managers typically have experience managing areas of the organization that have activities that need to be performed, human resources that need to be managed, and even department budgets that need to be developed and managed, but as we have seen from the preceding short list, effectively managing a project requires the manager to be experienced and have the tools and techniques to do much more than just the functional manager's responsibility.

- *Project management teams*—Another common area where the project manager experienced in project management might actually have some challenges is the development and management of project teams. Projects are first and foremost designed to utilize human resources to carry out project activities, and as all managers know, any group of humans required to do anything together will result in some issues or conflicts of some kind. Human resource management is probably the single area where project managers struggle the most because human resources are typically less predictable than other components of a project and difficult to plan around. In some cases, individuals might work exceptionally well on their own, given a project work assignment, but having to work with others to complete an activity results in a struggle for success.

- *Poor project planning*—Project managers have the responsibility to develop a project plan outlining all the activities and processes that will be required to complete a project objective. Depending on project managers' background and experience, and tools and techniques they have developed, project managers might not always be the best at planning a project. This can speak to the project manager's natural abilities. Some project managers are very good with the front-end development of a project and can develop excellent project management plans and strategies, but might struggle during the execution stage to oversee project work activities and manage resources. Other project managers might be poor at designing a project because they lack the detail and know-how to effectively plan a project, but are great at overseeing work activities and managing people.

  Unfortunately, in most cases, an organization will not know the specific characteristics of a project manager's strengths and weaknesses until after the manager has been hired and being given his first project within the organization to manage. The effects of poor planning can range from having only mild or moderate schedule delays or cost overruns, to severe or catastrophic problems causing projects to come to a complete standstill and running the risk of being terminated.

- **Human resources**—The issues that project managers face in managing human resource teams are very similar to those posed when the managers are managing individuals. Managing teams has different characteristics than managing individuals, although teams are made up of individuals; individuals act and respond differently in a team atmosphere than they might when working independently. Some individuals might work much better in a team atmosphere, whereas other individuals struggle in a team atmosphere but work well individually.

  - *Challenges with individuals*—One of the primary challenges in working with individuals is the personality conflicts that can arise and how this can affect the relationship of the project manager and the individual. Although friction might be apparent between particular individuals or between individuals and the project manager, as long as this can be managed, it might not have that big of an effect on accomplishing project activities. The project manager must understand that if difficulties are not managed with specific individuals, this can affect the project at any stage in the project life cycle. In some cases, certain individuals can create so much of a problem that it can jeopardize the success of a project or bring an activity to a halt. Individuals might even have strong opinions about how to conduct certain work activities or how the project should be run that can create conflict within the project staff and with the project manager.

Individuals who are borrowed from other departments within the organization might not approve of having been assigned to a project and might create conflict as a result. In some cases, individuals who are bored with their normal daily activities within a department might be excited to work on a project and might purposely extend work activities to delay returning to their department. The project manager must be cognizant of various characteristics of the workforce, as well as common anomalies that might occur, to plan an effective resource management strategy and be ready should these individuals display these types of behaviors on a project.

- *Lack of skills required*—Another difficult area in managing resources on a project is the assessment of skills required for work activities and comparing that with the skills of resources that are available. If resources are used within the organization, an assessment can be made with the functional manager and others who have worked with the individual as to the person's abilities and skills. If resources are contracted externally, this can be more difficult because the individual has not established a proven track record within the organization and the project manager might have to solicit information from resources the individual has performed work with.

When resources lack the skills to perform work activities, this can range from a minor setback in that an activity task is taking longer than it should, to catastrophic damage such that work activity was not completed as planned or with the correct quality, costing the project time and money. The warning to project managers in using internal resources is to watch out for the buddy system in which functional managers and coworkers have high hopes for a particular individual and that individual does not possess all the skills required to effectively complete a project task as required.

* *Subcontractors*—Just as using internal resources can have its pros and cons, this also is the case in using subcontractors, but subcontractors come with a contract to control certain aspects of the relationship. When project managers do not have a particular human resource skill set available internal to the organization, they are faced with soliciting external resources to fill this requirement. Unlike with internal resources, in most cases the project manager does not know a potential subcontractor, and this makes it difficult to ascertain skill sets, personality of behaviors, and general fit within the project team. Some of these items might be understood during the interview process, but in reality these characteristics will not fully be understood until the person has been hired and is working on the project.

  There are two important components that can influence a project during the project life cycle with regard to subcontractors: personality fit and skills set or abilities, and contractual issues. In many cases, the use of external subcontractors brings a breath of fresh air to a project and fulfills the contract requirements and expectations and in some cases even more. Subcontractors can also be an incredible detriment to a project, causing conflict within a project team and with the project manager, underperforming or misrepresenting their skills, or not being able to perform the task at all. In some cases, subcontractors fulfill most of their requirements only to use loopholes in the contract to get out of work, or acquire more money and in some cases create legal issues. These types of problems can have a wide variety of effects on a project, and project managers must be aware of the risks involved in using subcontracted resources.

- **Procurement**—Another important element that can have a huge influence on a project in the project life cycle is the area of procurement. Procurement is the activities required to obtain all resources, materials, and equipment to carry out project work activities. Many project managers will list procurement activities high on the list of potential risks that could affect a project. Most areas of procurement will be in the form of purchases, and as many of us know, purchases do not always go as planned. This can be a result of several aspects of the processes required to conduct procurement.

  - *Lack of skill or experience*—One area of procurement that can have a significant effect is the skill and experience of those conducting the purchases. Some purchases are simple, given a relatively common item that is easily understood by both the buyer and the seller, and can be easily shipped to the project location with a relatively low impact on the project. Other purchases can be very complex, requiring specifications or drawings to be interpreted, several options that need to be evaluated, and a challenging delivery that might result in damage, leading to a severe or catastrophic effect on the project.

    The purchasing agent lacking in skill or experience with complex purchases is more likely to make mistakes and therefore cost the project in budget overruns, schedule delays, and potential quality issues for the project deliverable. In some cases, the purchasing agent might be negotiating contracts even though they are not skilled in this area and again might have a legal binding agreement that puts the project and organization at risk.

  - *Too much red tape*—Depending on the size and structure of an organization, as well as the size and complexity of a project, procurement activities can be either easy or extremely difficult, depending on the amount of paperwork and number of processes required to conduct procurement. This is an area that the project manager needs to understand at the beginning of a project, to be aware of potential schedule delays based on the time of processing procurement activities. In most cases, this simply has an impact on the schedule, but it can also cause friction between the project manager or project staff and the procurement department.

- *Poor communication*—It's easy to blame resources in a procurement department for problems and issues with purchases and delivery schedules, but in many cases, this might be just a result of poor communication. Communication requires a connection between two individuals that will result in the successful transfer of information such that the receiver understands fully what the sender intended. Even the best procurement agents can fail if communications break down.

  It is always best for the project manager to assume the responsibility of good communication to ensure that project staff, other supporting departments, and management fully understand any communication the project manager is sending. Being that the procurements department will need detailed information specific to purchases, it is incumbent on the project manager to ensure that all the information required is effectively and efficiently communicated to the procurement department to avoid the risk of mistakes.

- *Challenges in procurement processes*—Most departments within an organization have processes developed to carry out the daily activities required of that department. Even if the procurement department has a highly skilled, trained, and experienced staff, working with a project staff that has impeccable communication, mistakes can be made due to poor processes being followed in the procurement department. This is not the fault of the project manager, but it can result in mistakes and failure within the procurement process that can affect the project throughout the project life cycle. The project manager must understand that if there is good communication and she is working with a great procurement staff, mistakes might still be made simply due to poor processes.

- **Project work activities**—One of the last major components at the project level that can influence a project is the work activities. One of the biggest jobs the project manager will have during the planning stage is developing all the work activities that will be required to complete a project objective. The success of work activity development typically is a function of the project manager's experience, but in some cases might have other influences that can present challenges in either developing work activities or carrying them out during the project.

- *Work activity development*—The first major challenge in an area that can present a great influence on the project is the development of the work activities in the planning stage and problems that can be encountered during this process. The project manager typically sees problems in work activity development that can include the following:
  - Incorrectly interpreting the goal of a specific work activity
  - Incorrectly designing specific work activity tasks
  - Underestimating the scope of a particular work activity
  - Incorrectly estimating costs for a work activity
  - Incorrectly estimating a schedule for a work activity
  - Allocating insufficient or incorrect resources for a work activity
  - Incorrectly placing a work activity within the sequence of activities throughout the project
  - Failing to perform an adequate risk assessment for a work activity

  As we can see, there are several areas where the project manager can make mistakes in the development of work activities that can have an influence on the project. During the planning stage, this influence can result in longer than expected time to complete the stage. In the execution stage, the project bears the effects of work activities incorrectly developed, incurring budget overruns, schedule delays, quality issues with the activity deliverable, and challenges with resources.

- *Too many problems*—Project managers should typically develop a risk management plan for all activities conducted on a project, but this important task unfortunately does not always get completed and in some cases is not performed at all. Many problems can be identified in each work activity at the beginning of the project, and response plans can be developed so that the project manager is prepared if problems are to occur. The challenge of problems within a work activity is when the project manager has not been proactive in properly planning for problems and as a result will have to be reactive after problems have already occurred. Even when there are multiple problems within a work activity, if the project manager has identified and developed responses for these problems, the response will entail simply allocating resources to carry out the responses. It is when the project manager is in the reactive mode, having no responses planned for problems, that a single serious problem or multiple problems can present challenges and can influence a project.

- *Work conditions*—Projects can vary in size and complexity as well as location. This can result in a variety of environments in which work activities are conducted, and this can present challenges and in some cases problems for work conditions. The project manager must again, in developing the risk management plan, identify risks relative to poor working conditions and develop response plans to be proactive in addressing these issues. In some cases, the project manager, after evaluation of certain working conditions at the beginning of a project, can actually develop alternative plans that might improve working conditions, eliminating the risk entirely. There might be conditions that are simply unavoidable that have the potential to cause schedule delays, impact the scope or quality of the deliverable, or even present safety hazards to human resources. The project manager must be mindful that poor working conditions can greatly influence a project, and anything a project manager can do to improve conditions would impact that influence.

- *Challenges with materials*—Another important area at the work activity level is the materials that will be used in the development of the deliverable for that activity. As materials were obtained by the procurement department, some of the issues might have resulted from incorrect purchases or damaged goods upon arrival to the project site. Some challenges with materials might be as a result of inferior product materials that will need to be returned for higher quality, causing schedule delays and possible cost overruns. In most cases, challenges with materials will generally cause schedule delays and in some cases are unavoidable based on shipping and delivery methods, storage of materials, and use of materials by the project staff. Materials issues can have minor influences on work activities or can result in severe catastrophic failure to a work activity deliverable.

- *Schedule conflicts as a result of delays*—As we have seen, there can be several elements within a work activity that can present challenges and problems, and in most cases, with issues concerning materials, this causes schedule delays within a work activity. Because most work activities require human resources, if these resources are allocated for only a specific time frame within a work activity, schedule delays can result in resources not being available, which compounds the impact of problems within a work activity. In some cases, this might be the result of critical pieces of equipment not being available as a result of delays within a work activity. These types of issues, in many cases, can be identified as a risk at the beginning of a project during the planning phase by the project manager, and responses or contingencies can be developed to ensure that project work activities stay on schedule. It is the project manager's responsibility to ensure that work activities are being managed to identify potential problems as quickly as possible, and responses can be initiated to minimize cost overruns and schedule delays that can also mitigate or eliminate schedule conflicts.

As we have seen, project managers have to manage their projects throughout the project life cycle with the reality of influences at both the strategic (organizational) and tactical (project) level. These influences can have a broad range of origin and can present challenges for the project manager that will test their abilities in all aspects of project management. Because these influences also can exist at various levels within the organization, the project manager has to continually be mindful of not only specific project work activity details, but also higher-level organizational and operations activities and general business conditions that might also impact their project. This is also why organizations will be more successful in managing projects when they have skilled and experienced project managers overseeing projects rather than functional managers or line supervisors. Because many of the aspects listed previously in both organizational and project level influences exist within regular functional departments, the project manager also has to understand not only this type of management, but also that of developing project structures, budgets and schedules, risk management, stakeholder management, and procurement management. The project manager truly has an important responsibility in managing a project throughout the project life cycle to ensure a successful outcome benefiting both the customer and the organization.

1.4 Life Cycle Models (Project Structures)

Organizations are structured based largely on the type of products or services they offer and how the organization manages connecting these products and services with their target markets. Because these products can vary in type, size, and complexity, projects that might be used to develop these products also have to be structured to accommodate each type of product or service being developed. For instance, a project structure used in the development of an office complex building (construction project) will be much different than a project used to develop a software package. A project structured for the development of instructional manuals that will be used at a government agency will be much different than a project structured for research and development of a future technology.

Project managers must be aware of the variations of project structures that exist to accommodate the development of various products and services and how these variations in project structures can establish different project life cycles. As we know, projects are defined as the development of a unique endeavor that is defined by a start and finish date, a time frame that also defines the project "life." Because there might be many types of products that can be developed and corresponding project structures, we can boil down these structures to four primary project life cycles. Each of these four types of project life cycles is designed to accommodate a particular type of project requirement in the development of a product or service and each also has a different type of management approach.

Linear (Sequential Process Development, Predictive)

The Linear project life cycle, also referred to as *sequential process development*, or "predictive" (a term used by the Project Management Institute in *PMBOK, Fifth Edition*), utilizes the traditional project management structure of a linear string of work activities connected based on necessity within a timeline and predecessor and successor relationships. The linear project life cycle is used for most types of projects in which a single project objective, sometimes referred to as a *deliverable*, is broken down into subcomponents that can be further broken down into smaller components. These smaller components are arranged in a sequential order that, when completed, can be assembled over the timeline of the project to accomplish the project deliverable. The linear project life cycle can be characterized by the following fundamental elements of structure and is illustrated graphically in Figure 1.2:

- **Goal (deliverable)**—The project goal, and output deliverable, is *well defined* at the beginning of the project.
- **Solution (project activity requirements)**—A work breakdown structure (WBS) of all work activities can be *well defined* at the beginning of the project.
- **Human resources (fixed or variable)**—Each activity, being a different component of a larger output deliverable, requires a *variety* of human resource skill sets and abilities.
- **Customer involvement**—Customers can be either internal or external to the organization, and the scope of involvement is typically conceptual development with the possibility of periodic reviews.
  - *Initiating stage*—Heavy customer involvement defining the output deliverable.

- *Planning, execution stages*—Minimal to no involvement.
- *Closing*—Heavy customer involvement for official customer acceptance.

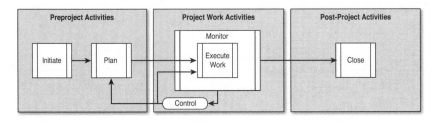

Figure 1.2   Linear life cycle model.

- **Budget**—When the linear project has well-defined work activities, budget estimates can be derived for all project activities.
  - *Development*—The project manager can develop a large portion if not all of the entire project budget within the planning stage of the life cycle.
  - *Management*—The project manager can manage each work activity's costs to an established project budget baseline throughout the project life cycle.
- **Schedule**—As with the budget, when the linear project has well-defined project activities, this allows the project manager to develop an entire project schedule.
  - *Development*—The project manager develops the project schedule during the planning stage of the life cycle.
  - *Management*—The project manager manages the schedule of resources, facilities, equipment, materials, and procurements for each activity throughout the project life cycle.
- **Scope**—Because the general project objective and output deliverable are defined at the beginning of the project during the initiation stage, the scope of the project as well as the product can also be well defined during this stage.
  - *Development*—The project manager and/or participating management and staff define the scope of both the product and the project during the initiation stage.

- *Management*—The project manager manages the entire project to maintain the scope of both the product and the project, as well as managing any changes to scope through a change management process.

- **Risk management**—Having a well-defined project at the beginning of the project, and a comprehensive breakdown of all activities throughout the project, the project manager is able to identify and respond to risks throughout the project life cycle.

- *Development*—The project manager can identify specific potential risks for each project work activity and develop a risk response plan at the beginning of the project.

- *Management*—The project manager manages risk responses throughout the project life cycle proactively in the case of preidentified risks.

Case Study Example: Construction of a Single-Family Residence

An example of a linear project structure would be in the construction of a single-family residence. The goal is the completion of a home that can be used by a single family as their residence. The solution is to break down the final deliverable into major components and then break down each major component into smaller subcomponents of work activities. The project manager can then develop a sequence of activities based on the logical development of how the construction of a home is carried out. For example:

- Prepare the initial groundwork for the creation of a foundation.

- Create the foundation in all the elements that are required underneath and inside of the foundation.

- Do the rough framing of the walls, any second-story flooring, and the roofing structure.

- Install rough plumbing, pull electrical wiring, and mount the primary heating and air-conditioning unit.

- Install windows, siding, and roofing.
- Install insulation and interior sheet rock and interior doors.
- Paint exterior and interior.
- Do the final finish of the kitchen and bathrooms, and install all electrical fixtures and flooring.
- Perform a final walk-through and gain customer approval.

Each of these areas can be well defined by the project manager at the beginning of the project, cost estimates and schedule durations can be developed, and a risk assessment can be made.

Incremental (Progressive Stage Development)

The Incremental project life cycle (a term used by the Project Management Institute in *PMBOK, Fifth Edition*), sometimes referred to as *progressive stage development*, is similar to the linear project life cycle in that the goal is well-defined, but project solutions might be developed or released throughout the project life cycle. The project manager still has the responsibility to break down a well-defined project deliverable into subcomponents; however, each subcomponent upon completion is released to the customer, and further development will proceed only after the customer has taken acceptance of each subcomponent and developed the requirements for the next increment. The project still stays within the original scope of the intended general goal, but the product scope can change slightly on each increment based on customer requirements.

The incremental project life cycle can be characterized by the following fundamental elements of structure and is illustrated graphically in Figure 1.3:

- **Goal (deliverable)**—The project goal, and output deliverable, is *generally defined* at the beginning of the project.
- **Solution (project activity requirements)**—Although the project deliverable can be broken down into subcomponents that can be defined, based on changes in scope or customer

requirements, each subcomponent might be subject to change and therefore the details of each component might *not be defined* at the beginning of the project, but developed at each increment.

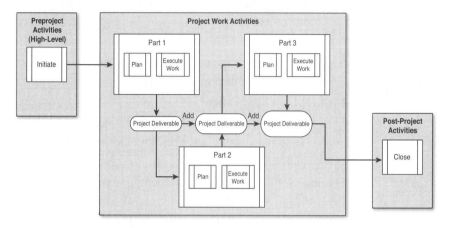

Figure 1.3 Incremental life cycle model.

- **Human resources (fixed or variable)**—Each activity, being a different component of a larger output deliverable, requires a *variety* of human resource skill sets and abilities.

- **Customer involvement**—Incremental projects have customer involvement both at the beginning and throughout the project as this type of project structure progressively develops throughout the project life cycle.

  - *Initiating stage*—Heavy customer involvement at the beginning of the project to define the overall general project scope and objective.

  - *Planning, execution stages*—Heavy customer involvement at each increment for customer approval of a completed increment and customer input for the proceeding increment.

  - *Closing stage*—Heavy customer involvement for customer acceptance and approval.

- **Budget**—The project manager, although knowing the general scope of the output deliverable, might only be able to produce a high-level budgetary assessment of the project at the beginning of the project. This is based on some information of components required for the main deliverable, but will not be able to assess specific details of each incremental part.

- *Development*—The project manager develops a high-level budget during the initial stage of the project, but details of each component are developed at the beginning of each increment.

- *Management*—The project manager manages the details of each budgeted increment independently.

- **Schedule**—Much like the budget, a high-level schedule can be developed to determine the general overall time to completion based on the estimated work activities, but this is at a high level and has a likelihood of change.

  - *Development*—The project manager develops a high level of the entire project based on the general conceptual understanding of the output deliverable, but needs to develop individual detailed schedules at the beginning of each increment. The project manager can also update the master schedule based on the completion of each increment, and the projection of a newly developed increment.

  - *Management*—The project manager needs to manage the schedule of specific work activities within each increment independently.

- **Scope**—The customer and project staff are only able to define the scope of the project in general terms based on the project output deliverable and this is subject to change based on the development of each incremental part of the project. The product scope will likely change for each incremental part.

  - *Development*—Project scope can be defined only at the beginning of the project and only in general terms, whereas the project scope for each individual increment can be developed more specifically at the beginning of each increment. The product scope is also developed specifically at the beginning of each incremental part.

  - *Management*—The project manager cannot manage the overall project scope or product scope, but does manage the specific project and product scope of each increment.

- **Risk management**—The project manager can perform a rough order of magnitude assessment of risks based on the overall conceptual idea of the project deliverable. This is based largely on the project manager and project staff knowledge of the general industry and the nature of the deliverable.

  - *Development*—The project manager develops a high-level risk assessment at the beginning of the project outlining common risks based on the general idea of the project deliverable. The project manager has to perform a risk assessment of each incremental part of the project based on more specific information within each increment and develop a risk assessment plan for each incremental part.

  - *Management*—The project manager is only able to manage risk and risk responses within each incremental part.

Case Study Example: Commercial Building Complex

As we have mentioned, the incremental project life cycle is similar to the linear project life cycle in that there is a succession of components, one built after the other. The difference is that the linear life cycle progresses virtually uninterrupted through a succession of work activities, whereas the incremental life cycle stops at each increment to determine what is required for the next increment. This can be illustrated through the construction and completion of a commercial building complex.

The general scope of the project output deliverable can be defined and initially planned as four separate commercial buildings created within a large complex that will include landscaping and parking. The project will begin with creation of the first building (first increment) and will be much like our example of the single-family residence, with ground preparation and foundation, tilt up of large cement walls, and installation of a roofing system. After the first building has been created, the parking lot, landscaping, and connections to the main access street will be completed for the entire complex for better marketing to customers, leaving only the large building pads for the remaining three buildings. The exterior of the first building "shell" will include finished windows, doors, and paint to entice customers for potential lease agreements. The interior of the building will be completely empty, having just the cement foundation floor, cement walls, and a roofing system with nothing else built on the interior. After the building has been finished, the project will stop, waiting for a customer to sign a lease agreement to use the first building for business. After a customer has been identified and a lease agreement has been signed, the customer (tenant) will finalize plans of how the building will look on the inside (offices, conference rooms, hallways, restrooms, break room, lobby areas, and any warehouse or manufacturing requirements), and the next increment will be planned for the build-out of the interior of the first building.

After the first building has been fully completed and the customer (tenant) has taken occupancy and moved in, the second building in the complex will begin construction, starting the next increment. After the second building "shell" has been completed, much like the first building, the project will stop until a tenant has been identified and plans to finish the interior of the building will be developed. This incremental process will continue until all four buildings have been constructed, customers (tenants) have signed leases and building interiors have been completed, and tenants have taken occupancy.

As we can see in the preceding example, the overall scope of the project can be identified at the beginning of the project, and certain components of the project, such as the four building "shells," parking lot, and landscaping, can actually be identified and planned at the beginning of the project. The variable component of this incremental project is the unknown aspect of each customer's requirements for the interior of each building. The owner of the commercial building complex (all four buildings and parking lot) decided to build only one building "shell" at a time and wait until a tenant has signed a lease agreement and finalized plans for the build-out of their specific building before proceeding to the next building in the complex. The incremental type of project structure works very well in this scenario in which there is a definite sequence of events that will happen, much like a linear project, but the customer wants to proceed incrementally based on individual customer demands for certain increments and risk management to ensure that each building has a tenant to provide revenue for the entire commercial complex.

Iterative (Features Addition Development, Agile)

The Iterative project life cycle (a term used by the Project Management Institute in *PMBOK, Fifth Edition*), sometimes referred to as *features addition development, Agile,* is a project life cycle where the conceptual or high-level goal is defined, but the steps for solution are not defined. The iterative life cycle can fall within a wide range of solutions varying from knowing most of the solutions to knowing very few or any of the solutions to accomplish the project objective. The features addition development concept of the iterative life cycle takes on the general form of developing process steps to create an initial output deliverable, and fine-tuning or adjusting the output deliverable to meet customer demands through repetitive cycles of similar development called *iterations*.

This type of project life cycle structure is typically used in software development intended for general consumer use sold through mass retail distribution. With this type of market condition, only a general concept of the output deliverable is known at the beginning of the project, and feedback from consumers is required to fine-tune the project over time. Each iteration of software improvement might simply be adding more features or in some cases eliminating bugs that were found and will pass through the same software plan and development process on each iteration.

The iterative project life cycle can be characterized by the following fundamental elements of structure and is illustrated graphically in Figure 1.4:

- **Goal (deliverable)**—Only a *high-level conceptual* understanding of the goal is available at the beginning of the project.

- **Solution (project activity requirements)**—Because the ultimate number of solutions and details of *solutions might be unknown* at the beginning of the project, after the details of design, development, and test verification are understood on the first increment, the steps will be performed on each iteration.

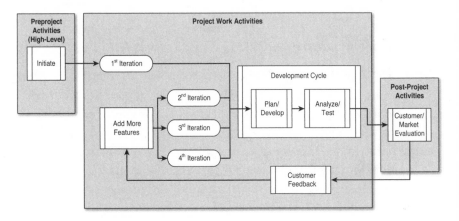

Figure 1.4   Iterative life cycle model.

- **Human resources (fixed or variable)**—Although the resources required for each step (design, development, and test verification) are *variable*, after the grouping of all resources to perform the steps in the iteration has been determined, resources for each iteration will *be fixed* and will repeat on every iteration.

- **Customer involvement**—Customer involvement is important and is what drives both the initial requirement as well as the ideas for additional features that will be developed during each iteration.

  - *Initiating stage*—Heavy customer involvement through market surveys and customer interactions to develop the high-level conceptual goal.

  - *Planning, execution stages*—Moderate customer involvement required only in providing feedback on features and improvements starting the iteration.

  - *Closing stage*—Minimal to no customer involvement required for release of iterations.

- **Budget**—Project managers find that creating a budget for an iterative project life cycle can be difficult at the onset of a new project, but are better understood after the first iteration has been completed. As the project develops through repeated iterations and these iterations are very similar in nature, the project manager can then fine-tune the project budget and begin to establish budget forecasts based on historical performance of a completed iteration.

- *Development*—The project manager typically develops a high-level budget estimate, and makes budget adjustments after a completed iteration.

- *Management*—The project manager has to manage iterations individually, progressively getting better after reviewing the results of a completed iteration.

- **Schedule**—Much as with the budget, the project manager can establish a high-level schedule based on a conceptual understanding of the output deliverable, but makes incremental adjustments to the schedule after a completed iteration.

  - *Development*—The project manager can only develop a high-level estimate of scheduled activities. The project manager adjusts the overall project schedule after a completed iteration.

  - *Management*—The project manager manages the schedule of iterations independently.

- **Scope**—In most cases, the project scope can be defined in general terms based on the conceptual idea of the output deliverable. The project scope, however, is more difficult to define because this is developed through iterations. The iterative life cycle for projects actually encourages product scope changes because this is what drives new features and improvements for the product.

  - *Development*—The project scope is developed at a high level with a general conceptual understanding of the project objective. The product scope can be defined initially on the first iteration, but changes based on customer feedback on future iterations.

  - *Management*—The project manager should try to manage the overall project scope to stay within the bounds of the development and improvements of the project objective.

The project manager must be able to work with several changes to product scope because this is the purpose and function of the iterative project life cycle.

* **Risk assessment**—The project manager typically assesses potential risks at a high level based on the type of project and output deliverable. In most cases, the project manager develops a risk management plan based on the combination of past projects that are similar in nature and the project manager's experience.

  * *Development*—The project manager develops the initial risk management plan based on the overall conceptual understanding of the output deliverable and scope of the project and product. Risks and risk responses should be similar on every iteration that is repeated. Additions to the risk management plan are made after the completion of an iteration, building a more comprehensive assessment of risk throughout the project life cycle.

  * *Management*—The project manager manages risk responses through each iteration independently, but should expect roughly the same outcome, and after assessing responses of the first iteration should be able to eliminate risks on future iterations.

Case Study Example: Flight Simulator Video Game

The iterative project life cycle is a unique structure that allows for the initial creation of a project objective, but incorporates a repetitive cycle of improvements to the product based on customer feedback. This is common in developing software in which the initial package of software code is developed and released for distribution to retail customers, and then after customers have purchased the software and used it, feedback is reviewed and the software goes through another iteration of design enhancements and improvements and then is released again through distribution to the customers.

In the case of a flight simulator video game, the initial game was developed and sold through distribution to customers. The video game included basic aircraft such as three types of fighter jets, one helicopter, and a transport aircraft, as well as a commercial jetliner, a standard single-engine civilian aircraft, and even an ultralight aircraft. The cockpit dashboards were fairly simple, giving the basic requirements for the user to fly the aircraft. Initial feedback from customers using the software indicated that they wanted to see a larger variety of aircraft and more functions on the cockpit dashboards.

The company applied these enhancements to the software through the second iteration and rereleased it through distribution to the customers. Customers expressed joy when seeing the enhancements, and included feedback for even more enhancements that would take the flight simulator program to a higher level of difficulty. Improvements then included several variations of fighter jet and military helicopters and other forms of aircraft. The game also included sophisticated improvements to cockpit dashboards and hand controls that would provide the user various forms of functionality. The software was released and customers were pleased to see these enhancements.

After obtaining more feedback from this successful flight simulator program, customers wanted even more functionality and sophistication to create even higher levels of difficulty. Through a third iteration, more sophisticated functionality and options and enhancements were designed, which included a 360-degree panning view, verbal and audible interaction with control towers and other pilots, and the development of actual missions through a mission control center for military operations. This iteration also included the capability to use the game online and interact with others over the Internet in the course of operation. Gamers could have dogfights and chase scenes in real time with others on the Internet, as well as develop an entire fleet of aircraft commanded by a central command in which everyone would be a part of a huge operation. This enhancement was then released for distribution through retail sales and it again became a huge success.

As we can see through this example, the iterative process allows the product to be released but goes through the same planning, development, and test cycle on each iteration, creating a better product for the customers. This type of project life cycle can span a long period but is considered a project because it has a unique output deliverable, and has a definite start and ultimate stop when the software is finally discontinued.

Adaptive (Learn and Build Development, Agile)

The Adaptive project life cycle (a term used by the Project Management Institute in *PMBOK, Fifth Edition*), sometimes referred to as *learn and build development, Agile*, is a project life cycle in which the conceptual or high-level goal might be only partially known at best, but the steps for solution are not defined. The adaptive project life cycle is similar to the iterative life cycle in that there are iterations of similar processes that are repeated, but with the exception that the repeated cycle is a much shorter cycle and there is generally much more customer interaction.

The second unique component of the adaptive project life cycle is that each iteration has not only an analysis and test function to be evaluated with the customer, but also a learn and build component that allows the customer and design team to build on each iteration as they learn how the product responds to each modification. Another component of the adaptive life cycle is a predetermined list of features that the customer is interested in including, but that can be added only as the product is developed and better understood. This features list is usually prioritized, and on each cycle features are added as a product technology is developed. This type of life cycle requires a significant amount of customer involvement in both the development and the test and verification components of each cycle.

The adaptive project life cycle can be characterized by the following fundamental elements of structure and is illustrated graphically in Figure 1.5:

- **Goal (deliverable)**—Only a high-level conceptual understanding will be available at the beginning of the project, and it is generally *not well defined*.

- **Solution (project activity requirements)**—A solution of the required activities is generally *not defined* other than just general forms of design, develop, test, and evaluate the functions in each cycle.

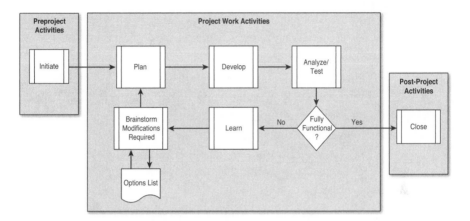

Figure 1.5   Adaptive—learn and build development life cycle model.

- **Human resources (fixed or variable)**—Due to the adaptive nature of this type of project, each cycle although similar in nature generally has the same human resources, but might add or take away certain specialized resources as needed, making this *both a fixed and a variable* human resource project structure.

- **Customer involvement**—The adaptive project life cycle has a significant amount of customer involvement at all stages of the project life cycle. This is primarily due to the "learn and build" characteristic of this type of project structure that requires customer interaction at all stages of the project life cycle.
  - *Initiating stage*—Heavy customer involvement responsible primarily for the initial high-level conceptual idea.
  - *Planning, execution stages*—Moderate customer involvement and can be at various stages of planning, development, and test verification.
  - *Closing stage*—Heavy customer involvement primarily responsible for the final verification and approval of the project deliverable.

- **Budget**—The adaptive project life cycle is difficult for the project manager to budget at the beginning of a project because little is known about what will be required throughout the project. If the project manager has had prior experience with a particular customer or type of project deliverable and the repetitive or cyclical nature of the adaptive project structure, the project manager might be able to derive some high-level budgetary estimates.

  - *Development*—The project manager is only able to derive a high-level budget at the beginning of the project, and needs to develop the budget throughout the course of the project life cycle.

  - *Management*—Due to the lack of project budgetary details, the project manager has to be reactive in managing budgetary costs.

- **Schedule**—Much as with the budget, in the adaptive project life cycle, it is difficult for the project manager to develop a project schedule covering the entire project life cycle. This is primarily due to the lack of information as to how many cycles will be required and how many resources in each cycle will also be required to complete a project deliverable.

  - *Development*—The project manager is only able to derive a high-level project schedule at the beginning of a project, and needs to develop the schedule throughout the course of the project life cycle.

  - *Management*—Due to the lack of details and requirements for work activities, the project manager has to be reactive in managing a project schedule.

- **Scope**—Because there is only a high-level and conceptual idea of the project deliverable at the beginning of a project, it is difficult to derive a precise scope of either the project or the product. At best, the project manager generally develops a high-level and broad scope for the project, allowing for variations in development and test and customer interaction. This type of project scope also needs to allow an open-ended number of cycles that will be repeated because the outcome and success of each cycle and state of product development will be unknown.

- *Development*—The project manager needs to develop a high-level conceptual project scope and likewise a high-level conceptual product scope based on the lack of information at the beginning of the project. The project manager can then make adjustments to both project and product scope throughout the course of the project.

- *Management*—The project manager needs to manage both the project and the product scope through a change management system. The project manager can also have regular customer reviews to evaluate the product scope and therefore modify the project scope to accommodate any changes the product needs to undergo to meet customer requirements and approval.

- **Risk assessment**—Due to the adaptive project structure and rather elusive nature of design, development, and test verification with high levels of customer involvement, the project manager should assume high levels of potential risk throughout the project life cycle. The project manager having experience with either particular customers or this particular type of product might be able to identify certain risks at the beginning of the project and plan responses accordingly. In most cases, though, the project manager can only identify certain obvious risks from a high-level vantage point, and must develop a risk management plan that incorporates the addition of risks through each cycle of the project or a reactionary plan that simply requires the best immediate response when needed.

  - *Development*—The project manager can only make a best effort in identifying risks at the beginning of a project, and needs to develop risk assessments and responses through each project cycle.

  - *Management*—The project manager, outside of some pulmonary risks that have been identified and responses that can be planned, unfortunately needs to manage risks in a reaction type of response rather than a proactive response through planning.

Case Study Example: Test Measurement System Software

The adaptive project life cycle is best used when a general high-level idea is available from the customer and certain features and functions might be included as options, as in the case of a test measurement system software requirement. For instance, an organization has a telecom product that can perform a primary function, but also has several lower-level operations it can perform. The customer wants to test the product to ensure that all functionality is operating correctly before the product is shipped to its final destination. The customer has requested that the test station be built where the product will undergo a series of tests to ensure that each individual function is performing as specified.

The initial discussion of this software package only indicates a very high-level conceptual idea of what tasks the software will be required to perform. Upon initial investigation, the design team, having discussions with the customer, has developed a list of functions the customer has requested and has prioritized by importance. The design team then develops an initial plan, on the first cycle of development, to build a source code platform that can extract information from several types of test equipment, process information from these pieces of equipment, perform various calculations that might be required to analyze and quantify product performance, and display the information from the analysis via a user interface.

The design team has determined that on the first cycle of development, they will build a source code capable of extracting information from the pieces of test equipment that are required, and build an analysis module within the software to process information from the test equipment. Upon completion of this task, the customer is asked to verify whether the information and analysis was valid and can be used in calculations that can quantify product performance. Upon test and verification of this initial step, the customer approves the initial source code.

In the next cycle, the design team then moves into the next phase of creating the calculations component and user interface output segment of the software. This requires several brainstorming and trial-and-error sessions of determining the validity of calculations being made. Upon completion of this segment, the customer is then tasked with the verification of the calculations and initial approval of the user interface. Upon approval, the design team now looks at the features and options lists that the customer has supplied to see what items can be added to the software package.

In the next cycle, the design team attempts to take the top two prioritized features on the list that the customer has provided and brainstorm how to incorporate these within the software package that has been developed. They meet with the customer to get more detail on what the features are intended to provide. Again, through trial-and-error sessions, the design team has been able to incorporate the first two features in the software package and again requires customer approval. Upon verification of these features, the customer has found that they would like to alter one of them, requiring the design team to yet again brainstorm and develop a solution and have the customer verify compliance and provide approval.

In the next cycle, the design team goes to the next items on the features list that the customer has provided, and again brainstorms how to incorporate these within the software package. They meet with the customer again to understand more details and what the features were intended to provide, and through trial and error they develop solutions that the customer can evaluate and approve.

As we can see in this example of an adaptive product life cycle, the same processes are used in each cycle, and there is heavy customer involvement throughout the project life cycle to assist not only in developing the features and functions, but also in validating that the software is working correctly and the design team and the customer are moving closer to an output deliverable that will accomplish the customer's overall conceptual goal. This type of life cycle works very well in accomplishing this type of project objective.

Extreme (Exploratory Development)

The basic structure of the extreme project life cycle, sometimes referred to as *exploratory development*, is a general-consensus-based starting point, and an undefined path of activities that will yield a project output deliverable that is only conceptual and also not well defined. These types of projects are typically found in research and development when only a vague general understanding of a goal might be all the project team is starting with. The project team is made up of various human resource skill sets and might change several times throughout the course of the project. The extreme project structure also has heavy customer involvement throughout the life cycle. In some cases, very little planning is done at the beginning of the project, and most of the project duration is spent in development and testing. There might be several points during the development when brainstorming and planning might occur, depending on what has been developed, and inputs from the customer for further development drive which direction the project goes in. The extreme project structure is a difficult project for project managers to design or quantify at the beginning of a project because so little is known. It's common for an engineering manager to be the project manager, simply overseeing all the research and development activities and coordinating with customers for inputs.

The extreme project life cycle can be characterized by the following fundamental elements of structure or lack of structure and is illustrated graphically in Figure 1.6:

- **Goal (deliverable)**—The project manager has *very little information* at the beginning of the project to define a project objective or deliverable. In most cases, the goal is simply a very high-level conceptual idea of a direction the project will go and is not necessarily a definable end result.

- **Solution (project activity requirements)**—The project manager also finds it difficult to outline a project plan and list of activities based on *little information known* about the project deliverable. The project manager typically is an engineering manager simply overseeing the progression of activities generally directed by the customer and based on the results of progress of a deliverable moving through the development process.

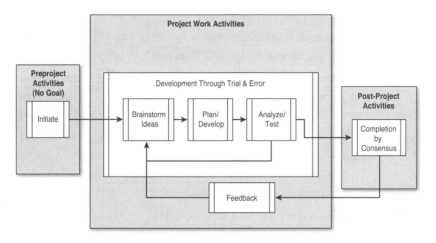

Figure 1.6   Extreme—exploratory development life cycle model.

- **Human resources (fixed or variable)**—Because very little is known about the work activities on extreme project structure, the project manager does not actually know initially what human resources are required for project activities. In many cases, the required resource is simply the allocation of research and development staff, which by definition might actually be more of a *fixed group* of individuals within an engineering department. Depending on how the product progresses through development, it's possible that a *variety* of human resources outside of the engineering department could be utilized at some point in the project life cycle.

- **Customer involvement**—The extreme project structure requires heavy customer involvement throughout the project life cycle. Not only can customer involvement drive the initial conceptual idea at the beginning of the project, but customers can drive and approve several directions of development during the project, having input and approval responsibilities and final approval at the end of the project.

- **Budget**—The project manager might find developing a budget of any type of detail difficult for the extreme project structure based on little to no work activity information. They very high-level budget number can be presented, but this has a high margin of error associated and typically is used only as a rough order of magnitude starting point for understanding the magnitude of the project relative to a budget forecast.

  - *Development*—The project manager only develops a high-level budgetary analysis with little to no detail. In most cases, this is used as a starting point for a project decision, making a long-range strategic analysis within an organization.

  - *Management*—The project manager only is able to manage a budget for an extreme project based on resource requirements within small elements of research and development.

- **Schedule**—Much as with the budget, the project manager has a difficult time scheduling a project that has no definable work activities identified. Project managers typically schedule inside of small segments of research and development activity.

  - *Development*—The project manager typically only develops a small duration of schedule activities based on small segments of research and development.

  - *Management*—The project manager also only attempts to manage small segments of research and development.

- **Scope**—Assessing the scope of both the project and the product is very difficult, because the nature of an extreme project structure suggests the wide-open brainstorming activity of research and development that can lead engineering groups into either one or several directions of development. The project scope must be sensitive to product scope changes in the direction of development.

  - *Development*—The project manager, although placing a very high-level and generalized project scope, has very little if any product scope input and therefore might not be able to define a product scope at all. Project scope is a function of the product scope and needs to change based on progress in the development of the project deliverable.

- *Management*—The project manager only is able to manage small components of product scope based on inputs from the customer in small segments of product development. The overall project scope is further defined as more of the product is developed, which is used to define the direction of both the product and the project.

- **Risk assessment**—The extreme project structure is one of the highest-risk forms of project structure that can be used based on several unknowns. The very nature of the project uses unknowns to encourage research and development, but this can also open the door for many risks as well as uncertainties.

  - *Development*—The project manager generally is not able to define much of a risk management plan at the beginning of an extreme project structure due to the lack of work activity information. The project manager uses the same strategy used in developing a budget and schedule, in developing a risk management plan in which small segments of work activity are analyzed and responses developed.

  - *Management*—Although some proactive planning might be available, the project manager manages risk primarily through reaction responses.

Case Study Example: Deep Space Propulsion Methods

An engineering group has been tasked with a highly elusive and futuristic concept of developing a deep space reusable propulsion system. If a customer requirement is communicated which reveals that the customer is interested in a propulsion system capable of moving an aircraft off of the planet Earth, deep into space, very quickly and returning back to earth, this might not yield an initial outlay of project activities to design, develop, and produce this type of propulsion system based on the lack of technology. The organization is compelled to take on this project based on the value of this type of technology being developed, but must work closely with the customer to understand the details of the propulsion system as the technologies are being developed.

The project starts off with a conceptual understanding, and possibly pictorial representations of futuristic-looking aircraft with propulsion systems that can move an aircraft very deep into space and back to earth in very short periods. This is a very high-level conceptual understanding of the overall goal of the project but has absolutely no detail as to how this will be accomplished, if it can be accomplished at all. The organization then sets out, again with inputs from the customer, to assess the capability of existing propulsion systems and determine whether the current system can be modified and used. Another direction of development could be futuristic research and development of technology that does not exist. This might require extreme out-of-the-box developmental thinking, propulsion physics, astrophysics, and possibly even quantum physics to understand how to solve this unique propulsion system design.

After several months of testing and evaluation of current technology and several interactions with the customer as to payload size and speed requirements, the first design team has determined that current technology is not usable and new technology is required. Although this first segment of the project has not yielded a project deliverable, the nature of the extreme exploratory development type structure was played out and a major question was answered as to the capabilities of current technology. This was an important step in the overall development of the propulsion system because this can now guide the design team in a more focused direction.

The second design team now focuses on areas of new technology development that the world has never seen. Several interactions with the customer are needed to fine-tune requirements of the propulsion system and possible aircraft designs. Because this is exploratory development, the nature of this extreme project structure encourages several changes in project direction and product deliverable scope, which also influences the overall project scope. The design team must undergo several forms of design and development as well as testing to gather information and, working with the customer, in understanding the evolution of a new technology.

Because projects do have a start and a finish, this type of project at some point will have a finish, whether it ends with the decision that the technology is simply not available at this time in history, or with the technology eventually being developed and the final solution for a deep space propulsion system being completed and accepted by the customer either scenario can define the end of the project.

The extreme project life cycle has a unique place in project management, in that although it does have a vague and rather elusive nature, it in some ways does have structure, and project managers can manage these types of projects. It is common for project managers to seek out structure and organization where the project deliverable is well-defined at the beginning of a project and the project plan can be outlined, including scope, budget, and schedule, as well as risk management components. The world of project management was designed to manage whatever processes are required to produce a unique product or service within a specified time frame, no matter how unique the product might be and what might be required within the specified time frame to produce the product.

1.5 Summary

Organizations around the world have a wide variety of products and services that need to be developed that align with their business strategic objective and maintain their ongoing success. Organizations manage the development of these products and services through an organized system of design and development called projects. Most products or services go through the same type of requirements, such as the concept and approval stage, planning and preparation, execution of work activities, and project closure. No matter what type of product or service is being developed and no matter how much is known about the project goal at the beginning of a project, all projects pass through a form of these four stages from concept to project closer.

Understanding the four stages of the project life cycle is important for the project manager. Just as there are many types of deliverables, there are also several types of project structures that can create this variety of deliverables. Project managers can become focused on the type of deliverable and lose sight of the bigger picture of how the deliverable will ultimately be accomplished. These stages can be rearranged in a different order; some stages might be of much longer duration than other stages, and some stages might not have very much work at all. The project manager must still understand that a project is born with a conceptual idea and this can be at varying levels of detail. However, some form of plan will ultimately be developed; work activities will be performed to actually develop, test, and verify the components of the deliverable; and, after customer acceptance and approval, the project at some point will be considered closed.

We have also seen in this chapter that there are five fundamental project structures that represent how the product moves through the stages of the project life cycle. These project life cycles include linear (*sequential process development*), incremental (*progressive stage development*), iterative (*features addition development*), adaptive (*learn and build development*), and extreme (*exploratory development*). It's important that project managers understand how these structures differ and in what applications they can be used because these factors can play a very important role in the success of designing a project. Project managers should also understand that within each one of these project life cycle structures, the project manager's responsibilities can vary depending on how much detailed information the project manager has at the beginning of a project, and depending on whether detailed information is not known at the beginning but will be available at other points within the project life cycle. This is valuable information for project managers in designing how to develop the overall project management plan relative to scope management, budget management, schedule management, risk management, procurement management, and stakeholder management.

Project managers should always seek out tools and techniques that allow them the best opportunities to succeed not only in developing the correct project structure, but also in managing the project throughout the project life cycle. Understanding these project life cycle structures and how they can be managed should give project managers confidence that they have chosen the correct structure for a particular project deliverable.

1.6 Review Exercises

1. Discuss the four primary stages of a life cycle. Contrast the differences between them.

2. Explain the difference between organizational (strategic level) and project (tactical level) influence. Explain two primary influences within each level.

3. Describe the project manager's role in the linear (sequential process development) life cycle structure.

4. Explain, in general, the incremental (progressive stage development) type of project life cycle structure and how the project manager would plan work activities.

5. Explain how the concept of iterations works in the iterative (features addition development) type of project life cycle structure. Describe the customer's involvement during this type of structure.

6. Discuss an example of how the adaptive (learn and build development) type of project life cycle structure would be used, as well as what the project manager's role throughout this life cycle would be in your example.

7. Explain the general concept of the extreme (exploratory development) type of project life cycle structure and how the customer is involved throughout this type of life cycle.

1.7 Key Terms

Project life cycle

Concept and approval stage

Planning and preparation stage

Execution stage

Closure stage

Organizational (strategic level) influences

Project (tactical level) influences

Linear (sequential process development) life cycle

Incremental (progressive stage development) life cycle

Iterative (features addition development) life cycle

Adaptive (learn and build development) life cycle

Extreme (exploratory development) life cycle

1.8 PMBOK® Connections, Fifth Edition

2.4 Project Life Cycle

2.4.1 Characteristics of the Project Life Cycle

2.4.2 Project Phases

2

Operations Management Processes

2.1 Introduction

Since the beginning of time, humans having particular skills that can accomplish certain tasks have been solicited by other humans to perform those tasks for some form of compensation, forming the basic foundational concept of business. A simple form of this concept early in man's history was in agriculture, in which individuals having the knowledge and the wherewithal to plant, cultivate, and harvest various food items could sell those items in a marketplace to other individuals. Some humans who had the knowledge and skills to build structures were hired by other individuals to build living quarters (housing), structures to manage sales of items (stores), structures to manage educational activities, and structures to house religious activities. In any case, individuals who obtain a skill and the knowledge to utilize that skill will find themselves in a position to organize work activities to accomplish a desired goal.

As organizations have developed throughout the centuries, the organization of work activities has also developed, in many cases through trial and error, into basic forms of operational structure that allow the organization to accomplish goals more efficiently. In most cases, organizations have more than one task that has to be done in order to accomplish a desired goal, and how multiple tasks are organized is important in defining how efficient an organization is at completing operational goals. Although the goal to create or produce something remains constant with most organizations, there are several variables in how to accomplish a goal, depending on customer needs and how the organization responds to market demands.

It is therefore incumbent on those with the responsibility of overseeing an organization to analyze its customer needs, market demands, and the types of products or services that will be generated by the operation to determine the structure of management and work activities that will most effectively and efficiently accomplish the organization's goals. In the course of this chapter, we will see how the work activities within an operation are structured for various types of customers and products and how the organization can use processes to consolidate and organize work activity tasks. We will also see in this chapter how projects fit within an operations management structure and the role projects can play in improving the effectiveness and efficiency of an organization's response to customer demands.

2.2 Organizational Structures

Organizations are typically created out of a necessity to produce a product or service, and because a wide variety of products and services are out there, a wide variety of plans can be used to structure an organization to accomplish their goals. Some organizations are very small and have only a handful of staff that can create a product or provide a service very efficiently. Other organizations have very complex products and require large operations to design, manufacture, test, and store products. Organizations that have multiple products, or have product offerings in several markets, might elect to divide the organization into large departments or divisions that might be located across the country or around the world. The primary emphasis in structuring an organization is to evaluate what types of products or services need to be created and how the organization will respond to customer demands for these products and services.

For the sake of efficiency in the terminology used throughout this chapter, we are consolidating the following titles: owners, board of directors, vice presidents, and any other executive staff considered to be within the upper echelon of the organization are being called *executive management*. Executive management typically is concerned primarily with two fundamental components of an operation: the *design of the operation* and the *management of daily activities* within the operation. The design of an operation is usually a function of the product or service created and the tasks required to complete daily activities to support the product or service. Some organizations offer products that require a manufacturing-based operation that has various departments to support a manufacturing type of structure. Other organizations provide more of a service type of product, such as construction companies that are contracted to build infrastructure such as buildings and highways, and they have an operation structured for that type of product/service environment. Organizational structures fall under one of three categories: *functional, projectized,* and *matrix.*

Organizational Structures

Organizations structure their operations based on the types of products or services that the operation is required to produce. Manufacturing and professional service environments typically have the traditional grouping of work activities to form departments, and these are called *functional organizations.* Organizations such as construction companies that have product/services such that the organization's resources are grouped based on each unique individual product deliverable are called *projectized organizations.* When organizations have more of the traditional functional organizational structure, but do carry out internal projects on a regular basis and projects are overseen by professional project managers, they operate as a hybrid of both the functional and the projectized organizations, and these are called *matrix organizations.*

- **Functional organizations**—Develop and maintain the classic structure used to establish managerial hierarchy with the organization divided into traditional functional departments. Departments can include accounting, human resources, purchasing, engineering, manufacturing, quality control, inventory, and warehousing, as well as shipping and receiving. Most of the work performed within each department is repetitive in nature and output deliverables are well defined and produced on an ongoing basis. The general idea with this structure is each department not only has a specific objective, but will have a clear chain of command wherein each department has a manager overseeing the work activities of that department. The manager of each department reports to a higher-level manager who may be overseeing several departments and the chain of command continues all the way up to the highest level of executive management in the structure.

Case Study Example

An example of a functional organization might be a company that manufactures several items for a specific market and provides these items for general distribution and sales. This type of organization will require an executive level of management to create the organization and oversee hiring managers to manage daily operations. The organization is composed of the typical departments, such as accounting, purchasing, human resources, engineering, manufacturing, inventory control, and warehousing, as well as shipping and receiving. The daily activities of each department support the manufacturing and distribution of products the company offers for sale. There is rarely the need for any large-scale projects within this type of environment.

Within the functional organization, special "tasks" are typically managed within each individual department and usually are overseen by the functional manager. These types of projects typically are small in nature, and shorter in duration, and the scope typically includes accomplishing process improvements and the creation or modification of documentation. Functional managers typically oversee these types of projects because they know what is required from the project deliverable, typically are considered a subject matter expert to outline project activities, and typically are the best individual to schedule resources within the department to complete the project objective. Functional managers hold most, if not all, of the authority for a project, and if project managers are involved they are simply an expediter for work activities. An example of a traditional functional organizational structure with work activities grouped into departments is shown in Figure 2.1.

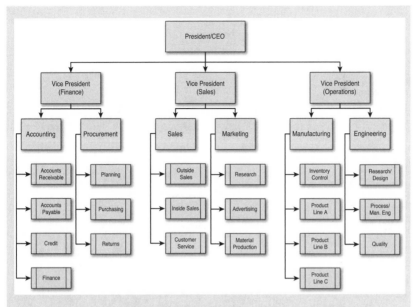

Figure 2.1   Functional organizational structure using departments.

- **Projectized organization**—Uses a completely different type of business structure than that of functional organizations; operational staff members are grouped into workforces that can include representatives from several traditional departments and are tasked with a unique project objective. This type of organization has only project groups and very few, if any, separate functional departments. Most projectized organizations were originally structured in this form as a result of their business strategic objectives. These objectives are based on groups of activities that result in unique output deliverables and therefore are considered projects versus individual departments that produce a similar output deliverable on an ongoing basis. Because the organization is primarily divided into project groups, it is typical for the staff on each project to report to the project manager, thus giving the project manager the authority over all project activities and responsibility of all the resources assigned to the project. An example of a projectized organizational structure of work activities is shown in Figure 2.2.

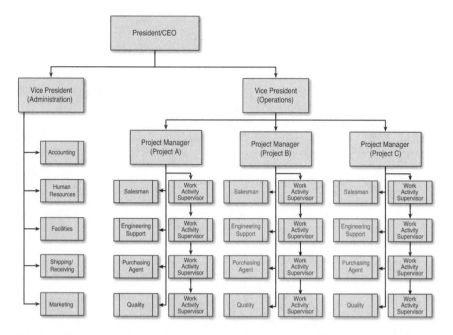

Figure 2.2 Projectized organizational structure of work activities.

Case Study Example

An example of the projectized organization might be a construction company that produces commercial buildings. Developers seeking the construction of specialized and unique commercial buildings hire these companies to manage the construction and completion of building projects. The organization, although typically having an executive management structure and possibly an accounting and HR department, groups specially skilled individuals to form a project team that to carry out all the activities required to produce a commercial building. Because the organization might have several projects underway at any given time, the organization also has multiple sets of the skilled individuals to carry out projects simultaneously. Because these projects are complex and have several phases of activities that have to be managed very carefully, the organization hires professional project managers to oversee each project. All the individuals assigned to each project report directly to the project manager.

- **Matrix organization**—Uses a blend of functional departments and groups of resources to carry out activities for specialized projects needed within the organization. The matrix organization has functional managers overseeing each department, but special projects required for department process improvements, engineering prototyping, new facility build-outs, or any other unique projects the organization might have are overseen by professional project managers. Functional managers hold the authority and responsibility of individual departments, but project managers hold an equal level of authority over individual projects and resources assigned to each project. An illustration of the matrix organizational structure of work activities is shown in Figure 2.3.

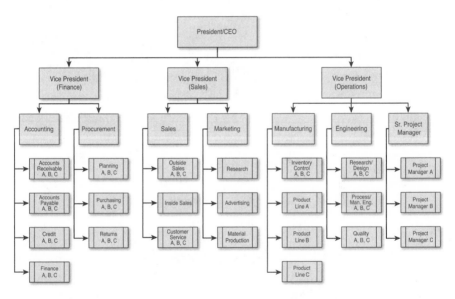

Figure 2.3 Matrix organizational structure of work activities.

Case Study Example

An example of a matrix organization might be a telecommunications company that produces specialized products for customers building telecommunications infrastructure. Unlike the functional organization in which generalized products are developed for mass distribution to a large market, the matrix organization has very specialized products for individual customer requirements, and each product requires a special project of developing a prototype for customer approval before mass production. A project manager designs a project and oversees all the steps required to complete the one-time and unique prototype (project deliverable). When the prototype has been completed and delivered to the customer and the customer has submitted approval, the project is considered complete.

At this point, the organization moves the approved product into mass production such that the functional organization produces the product on an ongoing basis. The project manager holds full authority through the development and completion of the prototype, but on completion of the project, the product moves into manufacturing, where the functional departments and department managers hold authority over the ongoing production of a product.

As we have seen, organizations have the luxury to structure their organization for the most effective and efficient use of resources to create products or services based on customer requirements and market demands. The three organizational structures previously listed operate very differently from each other, have different management structures, and produce very different products and services. Within each of these types of organizations, a management structure is required to effectively obtain and oversee resources to carry out daily work activities, and the success of the organization can be a direct function of the culture of management within the organization.

Culture of Managing

Whether organizations are functional, projectized, or matrix in structure, each has a unique requirement of infrastructure to carry out activities to accomplish the organization's goals. Each organization also has a structure of management that has been put in place to oversee the daily operations. It is this group of mid-level and lower-level management that needs to understand the vision of the executive management team and transpose that vision into an organized structure of activities that will accomplish the organization's strategic objective. In most organizations, it is the culture of management that can make or break the success of an organization. Mid-level and lower-level managers typically are responsible for many of the innovative ideas and development for specific operational activities. These groups of managers are also responsible for the overall communication within the organization, the management of risk and conflict resolution among managers and working staff, and the management of resources materials and equipment to keep operations moving.

As I've sometimes said, "Executive management is responsible for laying the train tracks in the direction they wish to go, but the mid-level and lower-level managers are responsible to keep the locomotive fueled and running down the tracks to get to the destination."

Mid-level and lower-level management is responsible for the daily operations of most organizations, and within the oversight of operations comes the responsibility of developing the infrastructure necessary to effectively and efficiently carry out the tasks of daily operations. Some organizations might have very large manufacturing operations with lots of automation requiring fewer human resources, whereas other organizations might be very labor-intensive, requiring only a minimal amount of equipment and facilities. Regardless of the size and complexity of an organization, all organizations have basic fundamental requirements to carry out daily operations. Organizations evaluating how to create their product or service within a given marketplace typically assess three primary areas that need to be designed and managed: *resources, work activities,* and *risk*.

- **Resources**—At the onset of developing a new organization, executive management is required to assess how the organization will be structured, determine what type of management will be required to oversee daily operations, and make a rough assessment of the overall requirement of resources to accomplish the objectives of the organization. In some cases, the founders of an organization start with a small operation, limited staff, a small facility, and limited materials and equipment. These early days of development are historic in the development of an organization because it will clearly be based on the vision, application of skills and knowledge, frugal spending, and risk taking of the original founders that starts the operations of an organization. Although this has been accomplished by thousands of people starting an organization, the ongoing success and development of the organization is highly dependent on how the organization is structured and managed. During the early development of an organization, the executive management is faced with three areas that need to be addressed for an organization to sustain operations and feed the growth of the organization: *obtain qualified staff, acquire facilities, and purchase materials and equipment.* Depending on how the executive management wants to oversee carrying out these three areas, they either carry them out themselves or employ managers to oversee the listed actions.

  - *Obtain qualified staff*—The executive management team starts by revealing the primary areas within the operation that need to be developed and managed, and this will drive the initial employment of managers to build these functional areas. As managers are hired, they typically work with the executive management staff to understand the basic needs of each department and compare those needs with the vision of the executive management for each department. Managers then assess more of the specific work activities required in their department and employ staff skilled in the specific tasks required within each department. Managers then develop a schedule of events to be carried out on a repetitive basis and hold the staff within the department accountable to ensure that all tasks are being completed on schedule and the department meets its designed objective.

Obtaining resources is not always an easy task, because individuals are able to articulate their skills, knowledge, and background only to a certain degree. Managers tasked with hiring individuals need to develop processes to ascertain whether individuals are qualified for the task they will be hired for. In some cases, this might be a trial-and-error type of exercise in which the manager might get lucky and hire a very qualified staff member at one point, but hire another staff member that simply does not work out and the manager has to replace that individual with someone else and start the evaluation process all over. It is incumbent on the manager to obtain quality staff because this will greatly impact the efficiency and quality of the department in general.

- *Obtain facilities*—Another form of resource that managers need to investigate is the acquisition of facilities required to carry out operations activities. This can be difficult, and in most cases requires executive management input and approval, but it can be vital for the success and growth opportunities of an organization. After a facility has been acquired, it is typically the responsibility of mid-level and lower-level managers to outfit the facility with all required equipment and materials, as well as staff, to conduct work activities. It is also the responsibility of mid-level and lower-level managers to maintain the facility to ensure that the operation is not at risk due to the impacts of facilities failure and poor maintenance.

- *Obtain materials and equipment*—Another form of resource that managers need to oversee is the acquisition of all materials and equipment required to conduct daily activities. After a facility has been secured, materials and equipment will need to be purchased quickly and set up and verified for operations. Because capital expenditure has been outplayed for the acquisition of a facility as well as the purchase of materials and equipment, it is the responsibility of mid-level and lower-level managers to get operations up and running as quickly as possible to generate revenue to pay for capital expenditures. Managers are also responsible within daily operations, to ensure that materials and supplies have been purchased and equipment is being maintained to avoid downtime of activities within the operation.

- **Work activities**—Although executive management is aware of the organization's overall strategic objective, and the basic design of the structure of the operation, it is typically the responsibility of mid-level and lower-level managers to design work activities and obtain staff, resources materials, and equipment to carry out all tasks required to complete the objective of the department.

Work activities are defined as all things that need to be accomplished on a regular basis to accomplish the objective of the immediate department.

Work activities can be conducted by automation through the use of robotic machines, or produced by human resources skilled, experienced, and trained in the task they have been assigned. After resources have been put in place to conduct work activities, it is the manager's responsibility to plan activities, schedule resources to conduct activities, and develop an overall cost structure to conduct work activities.

- *Planning*—Depending on the size of the organization, executive management might or might not be involved in the planning of what work activities are required for each department. In smaller organizations, it might be typical for executive management to play a very hands-on role in the development of each department, whereas in larger organizations, it is the responsibility of mid-level or lower-level managers to design the activities required within their respective departments. Planning work activities require the following tasks:
  - Design and develop what is required for each work activity.
  - Evaluate what resources are required to complete each work activity.

- Establish quality standards to evaluate the output of each work activity.

- Calculate the overall time frame the work activity will take to complete the task.

- *Scheduling*—After managers have designed work activities that will be carried out within their department, and they have assigned appropriate staff to conduct work activities, the manager needs to schedule how often these activities should occur and schedule staff to be available to conduct activities when they occur. Depending on the size of the department, this can be a very easy task for the manager or a very complex one, depending on the number of activities and staff available to conduct the work activity. Managers need to compile a list of all human resources and what skills and experience each person has as applicable to the activity each will be assigned. In some cases, individuals might be assigned several tasks and the manager has the flexibility to schedule any number of individuals based on availability.

- *Cost*—As work activities are being conducted on an ongoing basis within each department, the manager of that department will want to assess the efficiency of each work activity and the overall cost to the organization to conduct that work activity. The manager of each department should be cognizant of what the department costs the overall organization versus the benefit or tasks the department is producing for the organization. In some cases, it might be difficult to ascertain whether a department is a direct profit center (producing items that can be sold for profit) and therefore a cost-benefit ratio can be developed, or whether the department is in a supporting role and therefore is listed as operations overhead. In either case, it is good business for the manager to try to quantify what the department costs the organization, if anything, to try to develop ways to be as efficient as possible. The manager, after evaluating certain processes within the department, might find opportunities to improve processes to reduce cost and increase efficiency.

- **Risk management**—All organizations—regardless of size and complexity, what type of product or service is being produced, and whether they are for-profit or nonprofit—face the reality of potential problems that can impact operations. Problems can be classified in the forms of *uncertainties* and *risks*.

  Uncertainties are problems that cannot be foreseen or planned for under normal circumstances. For instance, "acts of God" events such as an earthquake, a flood, lightning, or wind are elements of our physical universe that have a tendency to strike without notice. Although technology is getting better at predicting when certain events might occur, these types of problems generally cannot be planned for and should be considered on certain events that have a potential of a severe impact on an organization's operations. These are also considered uncertainties, because the severity is unknown and therefore the overall impact on work activities also is unknown. In the case of an earthquake, the scope of this problem can range from a small-scale earthquake that might gently shake the facility, causing a brief stoppage of work with no damage to facility or equipment, to a large-scale earthquake that destroys an entire facility and all equipment and injures or kills many employees. Uncertainties have the potential for a wide range of severity and impact and simply cannot be planned for.

  Risks, however, are problems that can be planned for based on the assessment of information available that would suggest the likelihood of a particular problem under certain conditions. For instance, if a work activity is being carried out on a regular basis using a particular machine that requires regular maintenance and the manufacturer has clearly indicated potential problems if scheduled maintenance is not completed, the risk of failure on the machine is probable based on the manufacturer's indication of a specific problem due to a lack of maintenance. The manager can then identify the problem, identify the severity and potential impact the problem might have on a work activity, and develop a plan to mitigate or eliminate this problem based on available information. The manager can also derive a cost assessment to perform maintenance versus the cost of downtime and replacement parts and labor due to damage from a lack of maintenance.

The potential for problems exists all throughout an organization and at all levels within the organization, and management at each of these levels needs to be cognizant of potential problems that can impact daily work activities of their department. Although problems can exist at all levels within an organization, the ability to identify and plan responses for potential risks can present challenges for managers depending on what level of the organization they are at. Executive management has to deal with more corporate-level risk assessment and potential problems that can affect the entire organization. Mid-level and lower-level managers are more focused on potential problems within their specific departments and can derive a risk management plan for each department.

- *Corporate-level risk management*—The executive management staff generally includes in their responsibilities the assessment of potential risks that could impact the organization as a whole. This type of risk management is at a very high level within the organization and generally includes potential problems that most individuals within the organization will have little if any knowledge of. In some cases, depending on the size of the organization, there might be legal requirements for the executive management team to perform a risk assessment to ensure that mitigation or elimination plans or contingency plans are in place for critical problems to protect the organization. An example of corporate-level risks might include the following:
  - Lawsuits that could be served against the organization
  - Unexpected changes in the financial status of an organization such as the expected use of investment funding that is no longer available
  - Sudden changes in market demand leaving the organization with unusable materials or product
  - Irreconcilable differences within the executive management resulting in a critical executive manager leaving the organization

- *Operations-level risk management*—Mid-level and lower-level managers are responsible for assessing and managing potential risk within their respective departments. In most cases, risk at the operations level can be identified fairly easily, and elimination or mitigation plans, as well as contingencies, can be developed. Unfortunately, this level of management does not always consider risk management a part of their job, and if they do, typically they do not have time to perform risk assessment and develop a plan to manage risk. This level of management manages risk by simply responding to problems after they have occurred. At the operations level, examples of risk can include the following:
  - Problems with staff
  - Problems associated with equipment or facilities
  - Problems associated with product, materials, or supplies
  - Problems associated with miscommunication within a department or with other departments
  - Conflict between managers

The culture of management within operations, especially at the mid- and lower-level management positions, is to establish a structure of work activities and manage staff to ensure that the responsibilities of the department are met on a regular basis. This process for developing an organizational structure is typical with many organizations and has proven to be successful if implemented and managed correctly. Most departments will develop and document procedures and processes to control work activities and manage the training of new staff. The success of these organizational structures lies within the effective grouping of work activities that form departments overseen by functional managers. The focus of each department having the responsibility, collectively within an organization, allows the organization to be fairly efficient in accomplishing the organization's strategic objectives. This section of the chapter describes the basic foundation of how an organization initially develops an operational structure; executive management and mid- and lower-level management go a step further and create what is called a strategic approach and a tactical approach to managing activities within the operation.

2.3 Strategic and Tactical Approach to Operations

Just as executive management typically had a vision for the overall objective of an organization, mid-level and lower-level managers also develop a vision for their respective department or element of responsibility. In most cases, mid-level and lower-level management are not typically involved in executive management meetings and therefore are generally not aware of the executive management's overall vision of the organization. This is not necessarily a problem because executive management and lower-level managers operate at two different levels within the organization. Executive management operates at what's called the *strategic level,* and mid- and lower-level managers operate at what's called the *tactical level.* Executive-level management have either formed or know these two levels exist as they are generally formed as part of an overall business strategy. This allows executive management to deal with higher-level planning and issues of the organization, and separates the mid- and level-lower managers to focus more on the daily operations without having to be bothered with higher-level organizational concerns.

Business Strategy

Executive management, having a responsibility to design the overall structure of operations, develops a plan based on two levels of business operation: strategic operations and tactical operations. At the strategic level, executive managers are the primary designers and operators looking at the overall long-term goals of the organization. At this level, indications of market demands and market response strategies, product offerings and product mix to address market demands, decisions for research and development projects, and strategic growth initiatives are the primary concerns of executive management. Although the executive management team is responsible for ensuring that a tactical level of operations has been defined, it is the mid- and lower-level management structure that typically develops the operational structure, hires staff purchase equipment and materials, and divides work activities within functional departments to carry out daily work activities at the tactical level.

- **Strategic objectives**—This is the highest-level, broad-scoped, long-term planning the executive management team performs to develop future goals and a road map of what will need to happen to keep the organization successful. In many cases, the executive team members need to be visionary thinkers, developing plans for future products that might be required for future markets. The strategic objectives are developed to give an organization a platform for planning future growth, making an assessment of facility requirements, and evaluating required funding and lines of credit that might need to be acquired. At the strategic level, not many absolute details are involved in planning, but it comprises more of the grand scheme of forward thinking and planning of organizational objectives.

- *Founders vision*—The founders of an organization are typically the visionary thinkers because they are the individuals who have the initial vision to start the organization. It is these individuals, having developed a process and a knack for forward thinking, who typically come up with strategic ideas of what markets the organization might engage in. It is important that the original founders share their vision with other staff at the executive management level so that if the original founders ever leave the organization the executive management staff will understand and carry out the initiative set out by the founders.

- *Organizational directives*—The executive management team typically is responsible for instructing the mid- and lower-level management staff as to organizational directives, new plans for product development, and the requirements to change or alter operations to prepare for new strategic plans. It is incumbent on the executive management team to be timely in communicating changes of organizational strategy so that mid- and lower-level management can respond quickly and effectively to changes required in operational structure.

- *Market evolution*—As the organization has developed a plan to address market demands, it is typically the executive management team, along with marketing, that needs to develop plans to respond to changes in the market and how the organization needs to respond to those changes. In some cases, heavily established markets do not necessarily change as much as they simply evolve, requiring incremental improvements as the market understands change requirements. In other markets that are much more volatile, an entire product offering suitable for a particular market demand can see a completely different requirement demand or a market go away completely. This highly volatile market environment, with a very dynamic and constantly changing product demand structure, can be difficult for organizations to respond to, and can present challenges for an organization in fast product development.

- **Tactical approach to operations**—Mid- and lower-level management generally has the responsibility to design, construct, implement, and oversee operational structure and daily work activities. Mid- and lower-level management is not necessarily concerned with high-level strategic development or concerns, but simply waits for communication from executive management as to any changes or requirements needed at the tactical level. It then is the responsibility of the mid- and lower-level management structure to carry out the requests of the executive management team. Most organizations respond to market demands based on general product offerings forming the basic structure of manufacturing operations and departmental structures, or products designed for a specific customer requirement. Depending on the size of the organization and the type and complexity of products or services offered by the organization, two primary philosophies of work activity grouping exist within an organization: departmental work activity grouping and customer-based work activity grouping.

  - *Departmental work activity grouping*—When market demands define products in general terms such as consumer-based products and general industry-based products that can be produced in a manufacturing environment and distributed in high volume for consumer purchase, this type of environment generally produces work activities grouped by department. The traditional manufacturing environment,

as we have stated in this chapter, includes functional departments such as accounting, human resources, purchasing,
sales and marketing, engineering, manufacturing, inventory
control, and warehousing, as well as shipping and receiving. Each of these departments has a specific task, and work
activities are grouped into individual departments that collectively produce products for mass distribution. It is rare
in these environments that products are specific to an individual customer because this would require additional specialized work activities that the organization, in most cases,
is not prepared for. This type of structure defines the classic
functional organization.

In some cases, a functional organization can develop special
groupings of work activities that allow projects to respond
to specialized customer demands. Departments such as
engineering might employ project managers to oversee special development projects to modify an existing product to
meet a specific customer requirement. These types of organizations are structured as a hybrid in which projects can
be utilized on a regular basis, but are used only in special
development cases, and these organizations are called matrix
organizations.

- *Customer-based work activity grouping*—Organizations
  that produce a product or service specific to a customer
  demand will focus group work activities on the requirement
  of a specific product. This type of organization typically does
  not have traditional departments, but allocates resources
  throughout the organization to major projects and groups
  the work activities according to the needs of a specific project. The purpose of this project is to fulfill the requirements
  of a project deliverable based on the unique specifications of
  an individual customer.

Success Through Organization

As we have seen throughout this chapter, the success of an organization is based on the structure of its operations and how work
activities are developed and managed. In most cases, the real basis for

success is through the effective organization of work activities and the power that organization can have on daily operations. It really doesn't matter whether an organization is structured to be a functional, projectized, or matrix operation; what matters is the fact that work activities are organized, and through organization, daily operations are effective and efficient in completing the organization's objectives.

One of the inevitable outcomes of organizing work activities is the development and documentation of each work activity's specific tasks, and this is called a *process*. A process is defined as the "logical and sequential grouping of specific tasks required to produce a desired output." Processes are critical for an organization, especially in managing daily operations, because this is how mid- and lower-level managers ensure that work activities are conducted correctly and efficiently.

- **Operations activities designed as processes**—As we have learned, processes are a sequential grouping of specific tasks that produce a desired output. Every department within the organization develops processes to carry out work activities on a daily basis. Mid-level and lower-level managers have come to understand the power of organizing work activities into a systematic structure, and in some cases sequence, to effectively and efficiently complete the responsibilities required of their respective department. The fundamental idea of a process is the sequential organization of specific tasks, and functional managers take this philosophy to the next level in designing their department in the form of organizing processes to accomplish tactical objectives. Because this tactical approach to organizing tasks and work activities within a department typically works well with regularly scheduled output deliverables, functional managers struggle with the assignment of a specialized requirement that might require resources to perform work activities not typical of their department's normal function. This type of grouping of work activities would be considered a *project*.

- **Operations processes grouped as projects**—Functional managers understand the power of grouping tasks into processes and grouping processes of work activities into a sequential form that improves efficiency in completing departmental objectives. When special requirements call for specific work activities to be utilized in a way that is not typical of daily operations, this special grouping of work activities in the form of a project is another way the operation can utilize the philosophy of organizing specific task or work activities in the form of a process. When work activities are sequentially organized to complete a specialized output deliverable, it still utilizes the fundamental principle of a process, simply defining a different type of activity structure that might require specialized managerial skills. In most cases, projects are simply other ways to group work activities in an organized fashion to accomplish a specialized objective. Projects usually utilize organizational processes that have already been developed but are simply to be used in a specialized format and sequential order. Projects are sometimes referred to as hybrid operational processes, because they use normal operations processes, just in a different way.

- **Operations efficiency through projects**—As functional managers know the power of organizing tasks to form processes and how this introduces organizational structure within a department, so can the use of projects within an operation. The primary output of a process is efficiency, and as a process is developed, it goes through process improvements to refine details within the process structure to maximize efficiency. This is also the case in the use of projects within an organization in which projects go through a refinement process of evaluating the details within each process step to ensure that the project is designed for maximum efficiency. Therefore, projects take the fundamental philosophy of efficiency and process development and utilize it for specialized requirements so that the operation can respond to special needs.

2.4 Project Versus Product Management

In the course of this chapter, we have seen how organizations can be structured to accomplish strategic goals and objectives and how the tactical approach in organizing work activities plays a vital role in the success of completing a strategic objective. A primary component in the organization of work activities is the development of systematic processes to carry out specific tasks. Within each department in the operation, processes are developed to organize specific tasks and activities to accomplish departmental goals. We can therefore evaluate the structure of any organization in terms of a structure of work activities similar to that found in project management. An illustration of this breakdown of work activities within a department of an organizational structure is shown in Figure 2.4.

Figure 2.4   Breakdown of work activities in a department.

In most traditional project structures, the project manager begins the development of a project management plan by evaluating a customer requirement (deliverable) in its final form. The project manager begins a process of systematically breaking the deliverable into major pieces and breaking those pieces into smaller pieces until she has reduced the deliverable into the smallest levels of work activity. After this decomposition process, she can then align work activities to be completed in a logical and sequential form called a *work breakdown structure* (WBS). After the WBS has been created, the project manager can see all the smallest details of each work activity and can assess the requirements of each work activity, including resources, facilities, equipment, and materials necessary to complete each work activity. The project manager can then evaluate the cost of each work activity and the basic time duration required to complete each work activity. The project manager then manages each work activity to its completion, systematically accomplishing each portion of the work breakdown structure that results in the overall completion of the project objective. An illustration of how a project can be broken down into individual work activities is shown in Figure 2.5.

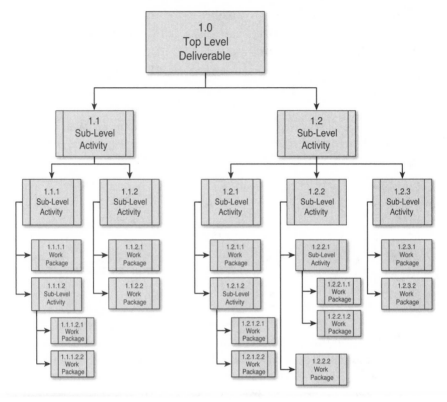

Figure 2.5 Project breakdown of work activities.

We can now see that the structure of a project in the systematic grouping of work activities to accomplish a specific goal is the same fundamental structure used in most organizations to manage ongoing daily operations. An organization having a strategic goal (deliverable) breaks down the deliverable into subcomponents and continues breaking down those components to the smallest work activities that are to be carried out on a daily basis to complete a departmental goal. Other departments are created to support the work activities required to produce the deliverable. At this point, one would ask:

"So what is the difference between a project structure and an organizational structure"?

The difference lies in the definitions of both a project and an organizational structure. Functional and matrix organizational structures are designed for the ongoing production of a product or service that is not necessarily unique because the product or service is conducted over and over and then continues until the organization deems that the product or service is no longer required. The specific components within the definition are the "ongoing production" of a product or service that is "not typically unique" but is produced in "multiple quantities," whereas the projectized organizational structure, being very similar to that of a project, has an objective to produce a "one time" and "unique product or service" and the "project will have a defined start and finish." As we can see, the difference in definitions is in having a *one-time and unique product or service* versus having *ongoing production of a product or service that is not typically unique.* Organizational structures are also designed to maintain production indefinitely, whereas projects have a defined start and finish. They are similar in using a systematic grouping of work activities and process to accomplish goals, but they are also different in how work activities and processes are carried out and managed. As we begin to understand and contrast the differences between organizational structures and project structures, we will begin to see similarities and differences, and through this contrast we can evaluate organizational structures and projects in terms of *project* versus *product.*

Organizational/Project Scope Versus Product Scope

The first component of evaluation is in the output deliverable required by a project versus a product produced by a traditional organizational structure. As we have already seen, in all cases, projects have a defined start and finish, whereas functional, matrix, and projectized organizations are intended to stay in business and produce output deliverables on an ongoing basis. In the case of functional and matrix types of organizations, these are typically like manufacturing and service-oriented structures that produce a similar product on an ongoing basis. The projectized organization is a special organizational structure designed to facilitate projects. The organization itself is designed to manage projects on an ongoing basis; however, each individual project has a defined start and finish and creates a one-time and unique deliverable.

As we begin the contrast of organizational structures and projects, we can start with defining the overall scope of a *project* versus the scope of a *product*. This evaluation is necessary to understand how project managers, as well as executive, mid-, and lower-level functional managers, view the *scope of an organization or project* versus the *scope of the output deliverable or product*. Scope is defined as the boundaries, limitations, and minimum requirements required in defining an objective. In our evaluation, we have two areas of scope that can be defined: the scope of an organization or project structure intended to carry out work activities, and the scope of an output deliverable required by an organization or a project.

- **Organizational and project scope**—When the executive managers and in some cases mid-level management, as well as project managers, *assess the requirements to produce a product or service*, which generally includes evaluating all resources, facilities, equipment, and materials required to accomplish the objective, this is called organizational or project scope. The important aspect of the managers defining this level of scope is to place boundaries and limitations, as well as establishing minimum requirements and what is needed to produce a product or service. This is the same evaluation carried out within an organizational structure as well as a project structure. All too often, activities are carried out with good intentions, but other work activities can begin to form that might not necessarily be in support of the primary product or service that will rob resources from the primary activities of the product or service. This can create problems in managing the allocation and scheduling of resources.

  Project managers have a hard-line rule to maintain the project scope because resources and timing of work activity completions are critical. In contrast, organizational structures also need to stay focused on the scope of work being performed to manage the cost of goods sold as well as general overhead. Organizations might be slightly different than projects, in that they can make a conscious decision to conduct sideline work activities within various departments and managers can employ staff to manage these extra work activities that typically benefit the organization indirectly.

- **Product scope**—Both functional managers and project managers have the responsibility to ensure that products and services that are being created are accurate to the original specifications required. Functional managers need to ensure that products rolling out of a manufacturing facility are being created as specified and up to the quality standards established by the organization. Additions or modifications to the product are approved and implemented only through a controlled change process. Project managers also have the same directive to ensure that work activities throughout the project life cycle are being conducted within the scope of what was required for each activity. It's the project manager's responsibility to ensure that the final project deliverable meets all minimum requirements specified by the customer, but meets only the requirements specified and nothing more unless the customer has requested a modification through a controlled change order process.

Organizational Processes Versus Project Processes

The next area to contrast between organizational structures and project structures is the development and implementation of processes. As we have already seen in this chapter, organizational structures have several departments and working components that all have processes developed to simplify, organize, and streamline work activities. Projects, also having groupings of work activities, require processes to ensure that work activities are completed on schedule, on budget, and within the quality expectations of the customer. A process is defined as a sequential order of tasks and activities designed to accomplish an objective.

- **Similarities**—Because both the organizational structure and the project structure utilize an organized flow of work activities to accomplish objectives, it is reasonable to say that both use processes to accomplish goals. Similarities between projects and organizations can include the following:
  - Both employ a manager to develop the flow of work activities (processes) as well as oversee activities to completion.

- Both encourage the evaluation and constant improvement of processes for effectiveness and efficiency.

- Both manage change requirements of a process through an organized change management system.

- **Differences**—Organizations and projects, although both using processes, can differ in the type of processes and how processes are implemented. These differences can include the following:

  - Organizations focus more attention on process development at the work activity level and not as much at the strategic or tactical level of management. Organizations use processes to maximize product efficiency. Projects, although utilizing various processes at the work activity level, place more focus on the use of processes in the management of projects. The project manager uses processes to manage work activity scheduling and resource allocation, as well as budget, schedule, and quality control of the overall project.

  - Processes conducted throughout the organization, although originally designed by mid- or lower-level management, are typically conducted at the work activity level by the workers performing the tasks. Processes designed for project management are typically used only by the project manager throughout the project life cycle.

  - Processes developed within an organization typically require subject matter experts, inputs from the workforce, evaluations by engineering, and a final approval by the functional manager for implementation. Processes developed for project management are typically developed by the project manager alone, or have been developed by a project management office director overseeing project management. In many cases, project managers might simply use industry-standard templates for project management processes.

Organizational Management Versus Project Management

The last area to contrast is the general category of management within an organization versus a project. The scope of this contrast and differential evaluation is at the functional manager and project manager levels. Functional managers are employed by executive management to oversee a group of work activities to form a product line or department within an organization. This grouping of activities typically has an output deliverable required on a regular basis. The functional manager oversees all activities within the department and allocates resources to ensure that activities are completed as required. The project manager is put in a position of oversight of a specific project typically by mid-level or executive-level management. The project manager in most cases has the responsibility to develop a project management plan of activities, allocation and scheduling of resources, and oversight of all project activities to ensure completion of an output deliverable accomplishing a project objective.

- **Similarities**—Because both functional and project managers within most organizations are at similar levels within the management structure, it is interesting to see, although they have very different responsibilities, how similar their jobs can actually be. Similarities of management responsibilities between functional and project managers can include the following:
  - General oversight of work activities performed under their supervision
  - Interview and selection of human resource staff identified for work activities
  - Management and development of staff within a team environment
  - Management of conflict resolution among subordinates staff, as well as other management staff
  - Scheduling of work activities
  - Responsibility for the completed output of work activities
  - Problem-solving tasks
  - Reporting of work activity status
  - Oversight of change management
- **Differences**—Because both functional and project managers have the responsibility to oversee work activities and staff identified to conduct tasks to complete work activities, how these work activities are structured and managed can be very

different between functional organizations and projects. Differences in management responsibilities between functional and project managers can include the following:

- Functional managers manage the same activities on a daily basis, rarely changing. Project managers have to manage many types of work activities over the course of a project lifecycle.

- Most functional managers are generally put into their position over an existing group of work activities (department) within the organizational structure. Project managers are put into position at the beginning of a project and have to design the entire project structure from scratch on each project.

- Most functional managers monitor and control departmental expenditures, work activity, and resource schedules, as well as the overall quality of the department's deliverable. Project managers, at the beginning of a project, have to develop estimates of all costs associated with every activity in the entire project, estimate time durations required for each work activity, and manage costs, schedules, and quality for every work activity throughout the project.

- Most functional managers do not perform a formal risk assessment of all activities within their department, nor develop a risk mitigation, elimination, or contingency plan. Functional managers typically operate in a reactive mode, responding to problems as they occur. Project managers identify as many risks as possible for each work activity in the project, develop an assessment of the severity and impact each risk can have as well as the probability of occurrence, and develop a risk mitigation, elimination, and contingency plan. Project managers, because of risk planning, operate in a proactive mode in which they are anticipating risks before they happen and making adjustments for risk elimination.

As we have seen through the contrasts and comparisons between organizational structures and project structures, there are many similarities in how the structures operate, in the products and services that are created, and in the responsibilities of functional and project managers. We have also seen these contrasts reveal some striking differences that set the project manager apart from the traditional functional manager. Projects have their place within an organization, and project managers assume the responsibility that the organization deems necessary to oversee a particular type of project. It is important for project managers to understand that projects are unique and are managed quite differently than departmental activities within a functional organization. When projects are utilized within an organization, there are certain interactions that need to take place to conduct work activities on a project within an organization. It is also important for the project manager to understand the importance of conducting work activities in conjunction with the work activities of functional departments and how project activities can impact the organization.

2.5 Project Interactions with Operations

Organizations develop an infrastructure based on the type of organization, the type of products or services that are produced, and the overall size of the organization, which includes facilities, equipment, and materials. Functional and matrix-type organizations develop the infrastructure based on the specific needs of each department. Projectized organizations typically develop an infrastructure based on the type of projects that are conducted and the facilities and equipment needed to conduct the activities of the projects. Projectized organizations are structured for specific types of major projects, and matrix organizations, although producing products or services, accommodate projects periodically as a normal part of the organization. Functional organizations typically have the hardest time accommodating projects, because it is simply not a part of their business plan or infrastructure.

For functional organizations, projects are viewed as something similar to a college student renting the basement room or attic loft within a house. They are fine as long as they are not causing any problems and generally stay out of sight. They will occasionally borrow the kitchen to cook something, use a restroom, or watch a movie in the family room that might impact the family residing in the house. Adjustments might have to be made in living conditions, and an occasional negotiation as to how and when to use something within the house might have to be managed. Functional organizations have similar issues in that projects that are not typical of the work activities conducted in the daily of operation are utilizing resources, occupying space within the facility, and occasionally requiring a negotiation of resources that might need to be used to conduct project activities. Although it is preached far and wide that projects are a good thing and valuable for an organization, one can't help but believe that certain functional managers are scratching their head and saying, "I'm not so sure about that—I can manage my own special tasks in my department, thank you!" Not all functional managers have had the opportunity to see the benefit of an actual project being conducted by a project manager and how it can benefit the organization. Outside of some extreme circumstances, most projects within a functional organization typically are small in scope and are confined to a single department where the functional manager oversees special tasks anyway. The problem lies not within the scope of the project, but within the abilities of the functional manager to design a special project, allocate resources effectively to complete work activities of the project, and see the project through to completion. These seem like simple tasks; however, although functional managers can start a project, it is difficult for them to stay focused on managing project work activities to complete a project.

As more and more organizations are seeing the benefits of formal projects being conducted within an organization, and professional project managers are employed or subcontracted to oversee the development and creation of the project, as well as the management through to completion, organizations must learn to accommodate project activities within their daily operations. When projects are conducted within an organization, such as a functional or matrix organization, certain departments within the organization usually are impacted to some degree. It is important for project managers as well as functional managers to understand the interaction between project processes and work activities and how they impact the operations processes and activities.

Human Resources

In all organizational structures, one of the biggest impacts that projects can have on normal daily operations is the requirement for certain skilled human resources for project work activities. Projects that are conducted in a functional organizational structure typically are isolated to a specific department, and the functional manager can allocate resources within that department as needed for project work activities. This scenario is probably the best case for projects to be managed within a functional structure, because the manager knows best which staff members in their department are most effective and efficient in completing specialized work activity tasks and can allocate those resources based on availability within the department. If projects are conducted outside of normal functional departments, and if they utilize resources from various departments, this usually has a severe impact on functional organizational structures because these structures typically do not accommodate project work activities and make scheduling of resources difficult.

Matrix organizations typically use projects periodically for various purposes within the organization, and departments are aware of the projects and have experience in managing the accommodation of resources being borrowed from several departments for project work activities. Although projects can impact departments within the matrix organization, the impact is not as severe because the functional managers have typically developed working relationships with project managers and understand the importance of lending resources for project work activities that will benefit the organization.

Projectized organizational structures have a slightly different challenge in managing resources for projects because the entire organization is structured for projects and resources typically are allocated to a project. Project managers have to be mindful of certain skilled resources being selected for work activities, because those resources will likely be scheduled on other projects and will have to negotiate and manage resource time allocations to accommodate two or more projects. In some cases, human resource allocation is actually the most difficult issue in projectized organizations because most of the resources are assigned to projects as their normal daily responsibility and are available only when they are finished with their work on each project.

Engineering and Production

Two primary departments that typically are affected by projects within most functional and matrix organizations are engineering and production. In most functional organizations, projects outside of an occasional product development are typically confined to individual departments and are used for process development or improvement for the creation or modification of documentation. In the case of product development, some functional organizations and most matrix organizations utilize projects on a regular basis to develop prototype products based on specific customer needs. Projects for product development typically are managed using engineering human resources, facilities space, and equipment and materials. In some cases, if the product needs to be tested for manufacturability or special operational conditions, prototypes might have to be sent to the production floor to be tested and verified using valuable production resources. Although this seems like an encroachment on normal daily operations, the project manager usually negotiates periods of time with the functional manager during which engineering can use production resources. As long as the functional managers and project manager communicate their needs and requirements of work cooperatively to negotiate accommodations, projects can be conducted within these organizational structures, and great things can be accomplished for the organization.

Facility and Equipment

Another important interaction that projects have within organizational structures is the use of facilities and equipment required for project work activities. Depending on the type of project and scope of work being conducted within project work activities, the use of facilities and equipment can vary greatly. Much as with the allocation of human resources for projects, project managers must realize that facilities and equipment have been obtained for use of the daily operation conducted by functional departments, and they must be sensitive to the functional managers, needs in negotiating the allocation of these types of resources. Within functional and matrix type structures, facilities and equipment will have been obtained for normal daily operations and might be available only under limited conditions for project activities. Projectized structures might have all the equipment and facilities required for projects, but the project manager has to schedule the allocation of these resources based on the requirements of other projects within the organization.

Procurements and Accounting

Two departments that might have interactions with project work activities are procurements (purchasing) and accounting. In many cases, projects have several things that need to be purchased throughout the project life cycle, and the project manager submits a list of these items to the procurement department so that they can be scheduled for purchase and delivery. Although this is the primary job of the procurement department, this department has structured its allocation of resources based on the operation's normal needs of purchasing on a daily basis, and the added responsibility of purchases for a project can present a challenge. A second form of interaction for the procurement department is the project manager's oversight on all procurements for a project to ensure that the purchasing agent has received the correct information and is making purchases in a timely manner so that deliveries will be made on schedule. This type of interaction by the project manager might not be typical for purchasing agents and the project manager must be mindful of this type of encroachment on their normal work activities.

The accounting department responsible for managing cash flow and lines of credit for the organization also is seeing financial resources being utilized for project work activities, and the project manager should be prepared to be held accountable should he be questioned about certain procurement activity. The project manager might have to solicit the advice or the approval of accounting for certain large purchases in advance so that there is no time delay when the purchase actually has to be made. It is the responsibility of the project manager to ensure that the accounting department has paid all required payments for purchases and outstanding contract obligations to ensure that work activities and procurements can be closed without incident.

Project managers should constantly remind themselves that their efforts in managing project activities to completion, and accomplishing a project objective on budget, on schedule, and at the quality expectations required, are a testament of the professionalism, skills, and knowledge base expected of project managers. Not all organizations are structured for the use of projects, and project managers should be aware of the impact projects can have on certain organizational structures. Project managers should also be aware of the importance of communication in effectively managing relationships with functional and executive management within an organization, because this is key to the success of managing projects within various organizational structures. Some organizations are actually including project management skills and experience in the job requirements of functional managers to build a culture of project management within the management structure of the organization. Other organizations that used to contract project managers for specific projects are now hiring project managers as full-time employees to manage any and all projects conducted within an organization. More and more organizations are seeing the benefit of well-run projects and how effective projects can be within any form of organizational structure.

2.6 Summary

Organizations have various structures of work activities and management based on the type of organization and the type of product or service being created or offered by the organization. We have seen that a primary influence on how an organization is structured comes from the vision of the founders of the organization and the work they provided in the initial establishment of the organization. An executive management team generally composed of the owners or founders of an organization, board of directors, vice presidents, and any executive staff that would be involved in high-level decisions of the organization drive this vision through the mid-level and lower-level management structure of daily operations.

Organizations are structured based on the grouping of work activities that form departments, and processes are developed to conduct all work activities required to maintain the daily operation of the organization. Mid-level and lower-level managers oversee work activities and processes to ensure that they are performed correctly and conduct process improvement exercises to increase the efficiency of each department's responsibility. Based on the type of organization and the product or service being offered by the organization, three primary types of organizational structure exist: functional, projectized, and matrix.

Functional organizations utilize the traditional organizational structure of work activities grouped into departments and managed by functional managers. This form of structure creates a hierarchy of management in which lower-level managers report to higher-level managers in this reporting structure, continuing all the way to the highest level of management within the organization. Because projects are typically conducted within a department by the functional manager, project managers within the functional organization typically are project activity expediters and hold very little if any authority. Projectized organizational structures are created when the organization, as its primary function of daily operation, performs large major projects for customer requirements and the organization groups its resources based on each product's requirements. When certain resources are finished on one project, they simply are transferred to the next project requiring those resources. The project managers within the projectized organization hold the highest level of authority because they oversee all the activities of each project. The matrix-type organizational structure is similar to the functional organizational structure, but uses projects on a regular basis for product development and special needs throughout the organization. Project managers in the matrix organization have a higher level of authority over the project, which borrows resources from various departments throughout the organization of project work activities.

We have seen that there are similarities between the processes utilized in organizational structures and the processes used in project structures, as well as very big differences. There are processes used by managers to oversee work activities as well as processes used within the work activity to perform tasks specific to that work activity requirement. We have also seen similarities in management responsibility between functional managers and project managers, as well as some very important differences in how these managers implement their responsibilities. As projects are used within organizations, and are typically not a part of the organization's daily operations, they can have an impact on various departments' daily activities and the staff performing functions within the department. Project managers must be mindful of the impact their project has within an organization and must develop processes, tools, and techniques to manage project work activities within organizational structure successfully. Organizations can be a better place as a result of projects, but only if projects are managed correctly within an organization's environment.

2.7 Review Exercises

1. Discuss how the vision of the founders of an organization affects executive-level, mid-level, and lower-level management.

2. List the three organizational structures and briefly explain the characteristics of each structure.

3. Describe what is meant by the strategic level of an organization and the tactical level of an organization.

4. Discuss the differences between organizational/project scope and product scope.

5. Discuss the differences between managing functional departments and managing project work activities.

6. Identify one department within a functional organization and how project work activities can impact that department. Describe how the project manager could improve the relationship between a functional manager and the project manager.

2.8 Key Terms

Executive management

Functional organization

Projectized organization

Matrix organization

Risk management

Business strategy

Strategic objective

Tactical approach

Work breakdown structure (WBS)

2.9 PMBOK Connections, Fifth Edition

1.5 Relationship Between Project Management, Operations Management, and Organizational Strategy

1.7 Role of the Project Manager

2.1 Organizational Influences on Project Management

2.1.1 Organizational Cultures and Styles

2.1.3 Organizational Structures

2.1.5 Enterprise Environmental Factors

3

Organizing the Management of Projects

3.1 Introduction

One thing that organizations have learned over the years is that a large component of success is based on the efficiency of using resources to complete the organization's strategic objectives. This is first accomplished in breaking down the organization into components of operations in which common activities can be categorized into departments to better manage and organize resources to accomplish the department's specific goals. The second element is to hire skilled and experienced managers to oversee each department to ensure that resources are being managed to conduct work activities that will accomplish the department's expected deliverables. The managers identify specific work activities and assigned resources to conduct tasks to complete these activities on schedule. The manager's responsibility is then to assess the overall goal of the department, divide work tasks within the department to accomplish this goal on a regular basis, and manage resources to ensure that work tasks are being completed.

Much like dividing an organization into departments and further breaking down those departments into work activities, the project manager performs similar processes when developing a *project*. Projects start with an overall output deliverable requirement, such as a product or service, and the project manager breaks down that deliverable into its smallest parts to assess all the specific details that have to be accomplished. The project manager is also able to estimate the cost and schedule of each work activity, as well as required resources, and the overall quality expectation for the output deliverable. Because an organization's success depends largely on the effective use of resources to drive efficiency in completing project work activities, so projects are also designed for efficiency by effective allocation of resources.

This chapter focuses on tools and techniques as well as processes in developing projects for efficiency. As some organizations use only projects to manage the completion of unique and specialized one-time objectives, organizations can also further develop larger-scale structures to categorize and group projects called *programs* and *portfolios*. We will see how programs and portfolios can also be used to help an organization accomplish its strategic objectives. This chapter also covers the project manager's roles and responsibilities given the assignment of overseeing a project, a program, or a portfolio.

3.2 Building Projects

In Chapter 1, "Project Structure," we saw how there could be different types of projects based on the objective of the project and the type of output deliverable. In Chapter 2, "Operations Management Processes," we saw how projects, much like operations, should be viewed as processes, and the project manager's role is to develop a project much like a group of processes. This is not to be confused with project management process groups, which are covered later in this book. The project manager should simply view each project work activity as a group of specific tasks that need to be conducted to accomplish the goal of each specific work activity. It is in the best interest of the project manager to view the project in components broken up into small pieces that can be easily defined and managed. After the project manager has the mind-set of accomplishing small pieces of the project at a time, he can begin the first stages of developing a project for efficiency. This section of the chapter is not intended to be a detailed explanation of all the tools and techniques used in the development of a project, but rather an overview of some of the simple things project managers can do that can be critical to organizing the management of projects. The first component of developing a project is gathering the information required to define the overall project objective, or as we call it *output deliverable*.

Gathering Information

The first task in defining an output deliverable, for the purposes of developing a project management plan to complete the output deliverable, is to understand as much of the detail as possible about the output deliverable. Some project managers who have extensive experience with particular project deliverables might be able to define a great deal of detail for a particular project deliverable. Other project managers who might not have this experience need to rely on other sources of information that are needed for the project manager to define the steps required in creating a project deliverable. The information-gathering process can be divided into two primary components: *deliverable decomposition* and *activity information checklist*.

- **Deliverable decomposition**—The project manager must first take the overall concept or primary output deliverable of the project and break it up into smaller parts to better understand the detail of what is required to create the project deliverable. This can be done by simply taking the highest-level output component and breaking it into smaller components, then evaluating each of these components to see whether they can be broken down even further. This process continues until all the components are broken down into their smallest pieces, called work activities, and this is where the project manager can see the smallest details of everything that is required to produce the overall output deliverable.

- **Activity information checklist**—After the project manager has broken down the output deliverable into its smallest components or work activities, a simple tool can be used to record information about each work activity. Information that is important to the project manager for each work activity can include the following:
  - What is to be completed at each work activity
  - A list of materials and supplies required for each work activity
  - A list of resources (such as human beings, facilities, and equipment) that are required to perform work activities
  - An estimate of the time duration required to complete the work activity

- An estimate of the overall cost of the work activity
- A basic assessment of primary risks that might be involved with the work activity
- Any requirements of other work activities that might be closely connected that need to be completed before the work activity can be started

After the project manager has captured the information previously listed for each work activity, she can get a better understanding of how each of the work activities is connected to the overall project deliverable and should able to develop a sequence of events to complete work activities in a logical sequential order. It is very important for the project manager to organize work activities correctly because some activities require other activities to be completed before those activities can start. Although some activities must be performed individually, one at a time and one after another, other activities can be performed simultaneously such that one activity is not dependent on others around it. After the project manager understands the characteristics of each work activity and can begin to develop a sequential order of activities, she can begin to develop what is called a *work breakdown structure (WBS)*.

Create a Work Breakdown Structure

After the project manager has all the details of each work activity, each of these activities needs to be put into a sequential order that allows activities to be completed in a logical order to complete the project objective. A popular project management tool for recording project work activities in sequential order is called the work breakdown structure. The WBS is a structure that promotes the identification of the smallest components or work activities required to complete a project output deliverable. An example of a WBS using MS Excel is shown in Figure 3.1.

As we can see in Figure 3.1, larger components of work activities are broken down into smaller units of work until the smallest unit or work package has been identified. The project manager can also assign a naming convention that can identify levels of work activity.

Another powerful tool the project managers can use to create a WBS is MS Project. An example of a WBS using MS project is shown in Figure 3.2.

Task	WBS Code	Project Task	Duration
1	1	PROJECT NAME	84 Days Total
2	1.1	First Sublevel Activity	28 Days Subtotal
3	1.1.1	Lower Divided Sublevel Activity	12 Days
4	1.1.1.1	Lowest-Level Work Package	7 Days
5	1.1.1.2	Lower Divided Sublevel Activity	5 Days
6	1.1.1.2.1	Lowest-Level Work Package	2 Days
7	1.1.1.2.2	Lowest-Level Work Package	3 Days
8	1.1.2	Lower Divided Sublevel Activity	16 Days
9	1.1.2.1	Lowest-Level Work Package	11 Days
10	1.1.2.2	Lowest-Level Work Package	5 Days
11	1.2	Second Subtask	56 Days Subtotal
12	1.2.1	Lower Divided Sublevel Activity	11 Days
13	1.2.1.1	Lowest-Level Work Package	4 Days
14	1.2.1.2	Lower Divided Sublevel Activity	7 Days
15	1.2.1.2.1	Lowest-Level Work Package	3 Days
16	1.2.1.2.2	Lowest-Level Work Package	4 Days
17	1.2.2	Lower Divided Sublevel Activity	37 Days
18	1.2.2.1	Lower Divided Sublevel Activity	27 Days
19	1.2.2.1.1	Lowest-Level Work Package	15 Days
20	1.2.2.1.2	Lowest-Level Work Package	12 Days
21	1.2.2.2	Lowest-Level Work Package	10 Days
22	1.2.3	Lower Divided Sublevel Activity	8 Days
23	1.2.3.1	Lowest-Level Work Package	5 Days
24	1.2.3.2	Lowest-Level Work Package	3 Days

Figure 3.1   Work breakdown structure using MS Excel.

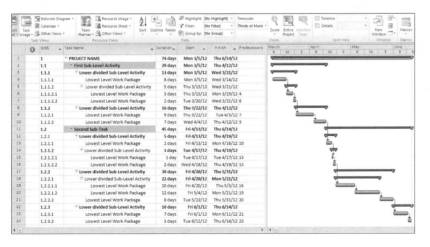

Figure 3.2   Work breakdown structure using MS Project.

The activity information checklists and the WBS are vital in establishing the basic information of each work activity. It is important for the project manager to seek out as much information as possible for each work activity because the planning phase of the project relies on complete and accurate information. The next component in developing the project plan is to analyze the relationships of work activities and whether or not certain activities rely on other activities. Project managers are not only responsible for planning and scheduling project work activities, but they must also be knowledgeable about the various interactions that might affect the success of project work activities. In most cases, the sequence of work activities is critical in how work activities are connected to each other within a sequence of activities.

Sequence Work Activities

The project manager is required to manage each work activity and in some cases activities being performed simultaneously. If the project manager is going to be successful at organizing how he manages work activities, he needs a tool to visualize how each work activity fits within the overall project. An important tool the project manager can use to evaluate the sequence of work activities is to align the activities in a form that illustrates how certain activities would be connected based on their relationships. This valuable tool is called a *network diagram*. Although there are several forms of network diagramming and lots of detail regarding how to build network diagrams, the emphasis here is on illustrating how the project manager can use this tool to organize managing projects. An example of a basic network diagram of work activities is shown in Figure 3.3.

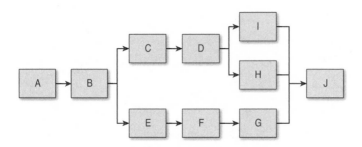

Figure 3.3   Basic work activity network diagram.

The network diagram can be a powerful tool to analyze how work activities are connected, whether one activity relies on another activity, and whether activities can be sequenced one after another or can be performed simultaneously. It is this type of detail about the relationships of how work activities are connected throughout the project that cannot necessarily be seen in the work breakdown structure. Because the work breakdown structure focuses more on the project manager's ability to break down components of work into their smallest pieces, and not necessarily any particular work activity being dependent on another or any particular sequence of activities. The network diagram is valuable in that activities have to be logically sequenced in order to move from one end of the network diagram, usually considered the start, throughout the project to the end. The project manager can then use the network diagram as a tool to effectively manage work activities in a logical order. The project manager can also evaluate resource allocation for work activities that might be conducted simultaneously.

When we consider the basics of organizing the management of projects, this starts with the fundamental structure of a project. Information that is captured about each individual work activity is important in developing project plans, such as the project budget, the master schedule of work activities, planning for potential risks, and the overall allocation of resources that are required to perform all work activities. When the project manager sets out to plan how he is going to manage a project, accurate and reliable information is critical, and simple tools like the activity information checklist play a vital role in capturing detailed information about each work activity. It is the project manager's responsibility to understand all the details required throughout the project and how work activities are connected to formulate a master project plan outlining all requirements to accomplish the project objective. These types of tools are basic in nature, but provide the project manager visibility of the smallest details of work activities. These tools will also be valuable in organizing how the project manager will manage each work activity individually as well as all activities throughout the project lifecycle.

3.3 Programs and Portfolios

Because projects are used to manage work activities for the purpose of accomplishing a unique endeavor with a defined start and stop, projects are typically focused on one objective or goal that will be accomplished. Projects are a successful way to manage completing single-objective goals within an organization. Even if the organization is structured for projects as their main strategy, projects are still designed to accomplish a single goal or objective. As organizations grow in size and projects grow in numbers within the organization, there will come a time when the organization will have to develop a plan to manage multiple projects. This can be accomplished through *program* and *portfolio management.*

Program and Portfolio Structures

Organizations that have multiple projects might find that organizing projects into groups can improve the management of projects. In some cases, organizations might have multiple projects simply because the organization is very large and has several business units that each perform projects. In other cases, organizations might have projects linked to specific customer requirements in which the customers might have multiple deliverables and therefore multiple projects. Organizations might use projects to develop prototype products and might want to group projects based on product groups. Regardless of how an organization uses projects, if they use multiple projects, grouping projects provides a more effective means of organizing the management of projects. We will look at two strategies of how projects can be grouped depending on the size and the needs of an organization: programs and portfolios.

A *program* is a grouping of related projects. Programs are typically used to group projects that have a relationship based on either a specific customer or a specific type of product or service. Programs can be open-ended, with related projects entering and exiting throughout the life of the program. Programs can have a start but not necessarily an end unless the organization no longer has need for projects within a specific program. Examples of this type of project organization are shown in Figure 3.4 and Figure 3.5.

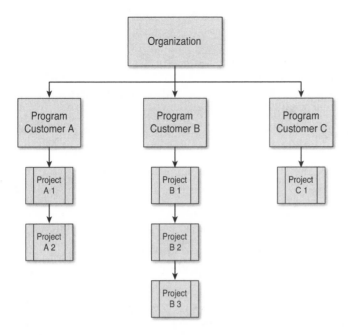

Figure 3.4   Customer-based program.

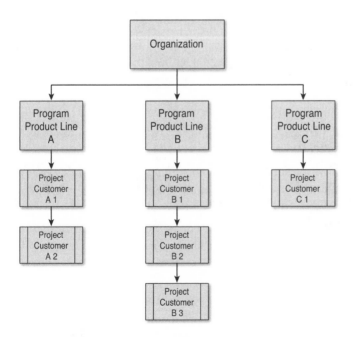

Figure 3.5   Product-based program.

The primary benefit to organizing related projects within a program is the capability to track the visibility of related output deliverables. In the case of customer-based programs, a program manager can monitor all project deliverables and can notify a specific customer as to when each deliverable will be ready for acceptance. Having one point of contact for all deliverables a specific customer has required from an organization is good customer service in managing multiple projects. Customers can also work with a program manager to adjust priorities on particular project deliverables and manage any changes specific to project deliverables through change management processes.

When projects are grouped based on a specific product type, program managers typically work with marketing or sales to understand time-to-market demands for specific prototypes. In this environment, groups of similar product prototypes are made and the program manager can manage schedules to provide completed products for sales and marketing strategies. In this environment, program managers are typically managing resource allocation, and similar products might require similar resources, such as human resources, materials, and equipment. It is also beneficial, when sales or marketing has to make a request for a change that might affect several projects, for the program manager to implement these changes under a more controlled environment when they are overseeing each project within their program.

A *portfolio* is a grouping of either related or nonrelated programs, projects, or individual work activities. Portfolios do not necessarily need to be specific to a customer or product type. Portfolios can also have a start but not necessarily an end, unless the organization no longer has a requirement for all activities within a specific portfolio. An example of organizing projects and programs within a portfolio is shown in Figure 3.6.

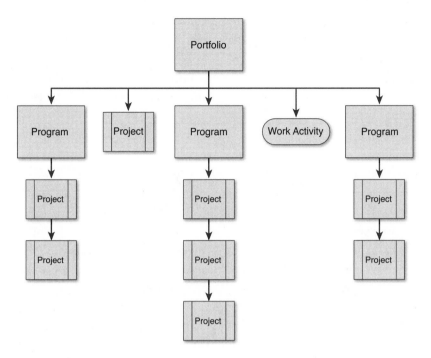

Figure 3.6 Structure of a portfolio.

Organizations utilize portfolios in several ways depending on how the organization has structured its operations. Some organizations divide up large components of their operation into portfolios, sometimes referred to as departments or divisions within the organization. In some cases, this might be customer specific or product specific, but in most cases if the organization is very large, each division or portfolio is an entire industry of products or services. Companies such as Siemens or GE are examples of organizations that have multiple divisions based on an associated industry. Each division has a portfolio of programs and projects that support products and services for that specific industry. Within a specific portfolio, programs do not necessarily need to be related because groupings of projects into programs can be managed based on various strategies within the operation of that portfolio. Portfolios can have programs, projects, and work activities that are all managed within the portfolio. Portfolios do require a higher-level executive type of manager to oversee all programs and projects within the portfolio.

Organizations that utilize projects on a regular basis find the management of projects much easier when they are organized into programs and portfolios. This is obviously the case when an organization has enough projects to group them in a logical way to manage specific customer requirements or product and service requirements. It's important for project managers to communicate to upper management the opportunity to group projects into programs and why this type of project management would benefit the organization. In some cases, project managers might find themselves creating a position for advancement if the organization accepts the idea of a program manager position to oversee multiple projects. Using programs and portfolios provides many benefits to an organization.

Benefits to the Organization

As we have seen, some of the benefits the organization can realize in using programs and portfolios is grouping of related projects and activities that can be managed within a program with a specific goal. When an organization is large enough to have several programs, projects, and work activities, an evaluation can be made as to the higher-level grouping of related as well as nonrelated programs, projects, and activities. Organizations considering the use of programs and portfolios can also find some of the following benefits:

- **Programs**
  - They allow the program manager visibility of all related projects and work activities for a specific program goal or objective.
  - The program manager can schedule the allocation of specific resources across related projects.

- The program manager can track project costs for specific projects within the program.

- Organization can assign one point of contact (program manager) for a specific customer-based program, improving customer service.

- **Portfolios**

  - They allow the organization to divide operations into logical groups based on multiple industries, multiple customers, or multiple product or service types.

  - Portfolio managers can evaluate the success of each program within the portfolio.

  - They allow the organization better visibility of smaller components of work activity conducted throughout the organization.

  - Portfolios give an organization with either a projectized or a matrix type of organizational structure the capability to establish managerial hierarchy.

3.4 Project Management Roles and Responsibilities

Organizations utilizing projects, programs, and portfolios will discover the need for a management structure that is skilled and experienced in these areas. There also is the need for the organization to establish roles and responsibilities in managing projects, programs, and portfolios. Most organizations that have functional departments have outlined what each department objective is and the roles and responsibilities of the manager overseeing each department. It is important for managers to understand their role and responsibility to ensure that the department is performing as expected by the organization. This is also the case for projects, programs, and portfolios, for which it is important these managers understand not only their role and responsibility but also their overall place of management within the organization. An example of the structure of project management within an organization is shown in Figure 3.7.

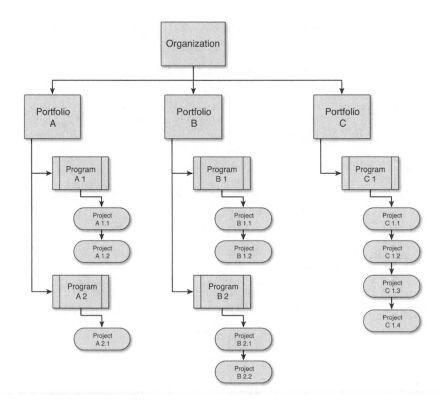

Figure 3.7 Project management structure within an organization.

Project Management

Managing a project requires the project manager to work with other staff within the organization and possibly customers to understand specific details of a project objective. Project managers manage the activities of a project at a tactical level within the organization because this represents the lowest level of work activities required to produce products or services. Project managers have a specific role within the organization as well as responsibilities in overseeing a specific project.

- **Role**—The role of the project manager is to manage all work activities required to accomplish a specific project objective.

- **Responsibility**—The project manager has several responsibilities in the course of a project life cycle, which include the following:

  - Work with organizational staff and the customer to develop a project charter

  - Using information from the project charter, customer specifications, and/or a statement of work, develop a project management plan that includes, at a minimum, the following:

    - Create a work breakdown structure of all work activities

    - Develop an estimate of work activity durations and formulate an overall project schedule

    - Develop an estimate of all costs associated with each work activity and formulate a project budget

    - Develop a quality management plan

    - Evaluate potential risks and develop a risk management plan of responses and contingencies

    - Develop a project communication strategy

    - Develop a procurement plan

Program Management

Organizations utilize programs on an ongoing basis, and in many cases programs are less specific in nature as projects. Because programs have multiple related projects and work activities, programs are used at a strategic level within the organization to manage either customer expectations or similar product or service groupings. Programs can have projects and work activities added and removed as they are completed, and new projects or activities are added to maintain the objective of the program.

- **Role**—The primary role of the program manager is to manage all activities required to meet the expectations of a program objective.

- **Responsibility**—The program manager oversees multiple project managers managing projects and work activities within a specific program. The specific daily management responsibilities can include the following:

- Evaluate which projects are added to a program to ensure that each project adds value to the program
- Select project managers to oversee specific projects
- Develop a reporting structure to acquire information for individual project status
- Evaluate the success of each project within the program and oversee the affective termination of unsuccessful projects within the program
- Provide mentoring and training for project managers within the program
- Develop a master cost structure of all projects operating within the program
- Maintain a master schedule of each project and the requirement of critical resource allocations across projects within a program
- Manage conflict resolution between project managers within the program
- Manage customer or stakeholder expectations based on the ongoing success of a program

Portfolio Management

If an organization determines that an operations strategy dictates the creation of portfolios to manage business activities, this is at a higher level than projects and programs and generally requires an executive-type management resource. In some cases, organizations have created a portfolio grouping of programs and projects similar to that of a division of the company, whereas other organizations simply have portfolios as a higher-level form of project management and not as a formal structured part of the organization. Regardless of how the organization utilizes portfolios, the role and responsibilities of the portfolio manager are as detailed here:

- **Role**—The primary role of the portfolio manager is to ensure that the objectives of the portfolio are carried out and meet the expectations of the customers and the organization.

- **Responsibility**—The portfolio manager must manage all program and project managers, as well as oversee work activities conducted on an ongoing basis. Specific ongoing responsibilities might include the following:

  - Work with executive staff on portfolio strategic planning and development of portfolio objectives

  - Evaluate which programs, projects, and work activities are to be utilized within a portfolio.

  - Select managers to oversee programs, projects, and work activities conducted within the portfolio

  - Develop a reporting structure to effectively and accurately gather information on program, project, and work activity status

  - Evaluate the success of programs, projects, and work activities conducted within the portfolio

  - Develop and maintain a cost structure of all programs, projects, and work activities conducted within the portfolio

  - Develop and maintain an ongoing schedule of programs, projects, and work activities to manage resource allocations

  - Develop a communications plan to manage the information of the portfolios' success with customers as well as organizational stakeholders

3.5 Summary

As organizations grow and mature, one thing becomes evident fairly quickly, and that is the power of organizing operations for efficiency. Regardless of how organizations are structured, the use of projects in the organization of how projects are managed can become critical if not managed correctly. Inasmuch as project managers can organize the activities of a project, we have found that there is a science in organizing the management of projects and how this can play a vital role in the efficient use of projects within an organization.

We discovered the importance, at the project level, of basic organizational tasks for projects such as information gathering using a work breakdown structure. Correctly sequencing activities using a network diagram can also be important. Although these are used by the project manager in developing a project, these are equally important as tools and in how the project manager manages a project. This chapter focuses on the organization of information, tools, and techniques used to manage projects within an organization. There is a lot written about how to build a project, but this chapter focuses on how to manage a project and the importance of having effective tools that the project manager can use to manage work activities throughout a project life cycle.

Another important organizational tool to effectively manage projects is that when organizations have multiple projects, these can be grouped into programs and portfolios. Organizations that use projects for the development of specific customer requirements or prototype products for specific markets can group related projects into a program that can be managed by a program manager. This is an effective organizational tool because the program manager can now focus on the success of multiple projects and how this translates into customer service in effectively managing customer expectations. Program managers can also more effectively manage resources across like projects and manage critical resources for specific timing across multiple projects.

If the organization has multiple programs and other related or nonrelated projects, a next-level-higher organizational tool to manage projects is to group programs and projects into portfolios. Portfolios are similar as programs, with the primary difference being that portfolios can have both related and nonrelated programs and projects as well as work activities within a single portfolio. The portfolio manager has a responsibility to manage all activities within the portfolio to ensure that the portfolio objective is being met and the portfolio objective is satisfying customer or stakeholder expectations. The use of simple organizational tools to manage the activities of a project as well as the use of programs and portfolios is how organizations streamline the effective use of resources. These tools are also used by the organization to effectively categorize and group various business activities for better visibility, accountability, and ultimately customer service.

3.6 Review Exercises

1. Discuss key organizational tools used in developing projects and how they are used in organizing the management of projects.

2. Explain how a program is used in organizing the management of projects.

3. Discuss some of the ways an organization can use portfolio management and how this is used as an organizational tool to manage projects and programs.

4. Explain the difference in roles responsibilities of a project manager and a program manager.

5. Explain what level a portfolio manager would be at within most organizations, and the importance of the portfolio manager's responsibilities within the organization.

3.7 Key Terms

Projects

Programs

Portfolios

Deliverable decomposition

Activity information checklist

Work breakdown structure (WBS)

Network diagram

3.8 PMBOK Connections, Fifth Edition

1.2 What Is a Project?

1.2.1 The Relationships Among Portfolios, Programs, and Projects

1.3 What Is Project Management?

1.4 Relationships Among Portfolio Management, Program Management, Project Management, and Organizational Project Management

1.4.1 Program Management

1.4.2 Portfolio Management

1.4.3 Projects and Strategic Planning

1.7 Role of the Project Manager

1.7.1 Responsibilities and Competencies of the Project Manager

3.9 Case Study

TCX Construction is a family-owned company that has been in business for over 40 years specializing in the construction of custom single-family homes. The organization has a small office complex for administrative staff, and project support staff such as buyers, planners, engineers, and drafters, that resides on a four-acre commercial property lot on the edge of a major metropolitan city. The primary use of this property is to house all the construction equipment as well as building materials and supplies. The organization has two primary divisions, commercial and custom residential, each led by a division manager. The commercial division has three project teams, each led by a project manager, that focus on the construction of large commercial property. The custom residential division is composed of four project teams, each led by a project manager, that focus on building custom residential homes. Each division has its own staff specialized in several aspects of the construction process. The division managers, in conjunction with project managers, allocate staff across projects based on the staggered schedule of each project and where staff will be utilized.

TCX Construction has been contracted to build a single-family residence in the foothills outside of the city. This custom home will be a single-story, 9,000-square-foot Mediterranean-style residence with six bedrooms, four bathrooms, a large den, a gourmet kitchen, a game room, and an executive office. It will also include a four-car garage, as well as an RV garage and a parking pad. The front yard will be fully landscaped with circle driveway and fountain, and the backyard will be fully landscaped with covered patio, outdoor kitchen, built-in pool, and spa, as well as a lighted tennis court. This custom family residence will be located on a two-acre parcel on the side of a foothill overlooking the valley floor.

3.10 Case Study Questions and Exercise

1. Based on a TCX Construction case study, gather information and create a WBS of major areas of construction, and break down these major areas into smaller components of actual work activities.

2. Based on the WBS that has been created, sequence the activities in a network diagram to form a logical chain of events to complete this project.

3. Explain how this organization can be broken up into programs and projects, and how these structures can benefit the company as an organizational tool.

4

Project Management Processes

4.1 Introduction

For decades, organizations have worked to improve the efficiency of resources utilized throughout the organization to produce a product or service to offer within the marketplace. Organizational structures can vary based on the type of business your organization is conducting, the products and services they are producing, and the overall size and complexity of the organization. Despite these various aspects of an organization, all organizations have tasks that need to be completed to carry out the objectives of the organization. And as long as an organization has tasks that have to be completed, there will be an opportunity to improve what the tasks are, how they are conducted, and in what structure of organization tasks are placed for highest efficiency. The first level of improvement an organization can make is to identify specific tasks for a work activity and develop a sequential order of tasks that would represent the most logical and efficient way to complete a work activity. This is called a *process*.

The Project Management Institute, in its publication *A Guide to the Project Management Body of Knowledge (PMBOK), Fifth Edition*, defines a process this way:

"A process is a set of interrelated actions and activities performed to create a pre-specified product, service, or result."

One of the fundamental principles in addressing workplace efficiency is the evaluation of how organized things are. Although this might seem a simple philosophy, millions of dollars have been saved when organizations have evaluated how daily operations are structured, how facilities and equipment are used, and how the allocation of resources is organized if at all. In some cases, upper management assumes that the operational structure is well organized and is running smoothly, when in fact, in some cases, this couldn't be further from the truth. When an organization understands the importance of a highly organized operation and the value this can bring, a culture of organized thinking begins to develop within the management structure. Although there is inevitably certain management staff who are highly organized by their nature and the organization benefits from their individual organized style of management, the organization does not fully realize the benefit of a highly organized operation until all the managers at each level understand the importance of being organized.

The primary output of a highly organized operation is the development of processes in which the tasks of daily operations have been systematically organized into logical process steps that can be evaluated for their efficiency and effectiveness. After processes have been developed, they can be evaluated and improved to further streamline how the process is conducted. A culture of organization within the management structure encourages managers to insist on process development and constant improvement. Just as this is important for functional managers overseeing work activities within their functional departments, this is also the case with project managers overseeing the work activities required to complete a project objective. The same holds true with project managers in that they are most effective when they understand the culture of the organization and develop processes to streamline their efficiency in not only managing project processes, but in the completion of a project deliverable.

The project manager plays an integral role in the development of processes for a project. There are two applications of process development the project manager will utilize for project efficiency: *project management processes* and *project work activity processes*, sometimes referred to as *product processes*. In just about all cases, the project manager is primarily responsible for the development of the project management plan, which includes all aspects of the project including the application of project management processes; it also is the project manager's responsibility to evaluate project work activities for efficiency and opportunities for process development.

Depending on the size and complexity of a project, smaller, more simplified projects typically have the project manager overseeing each individual work activity. The project manager in this capacity can have a direct influence on how work activity is structured and identify whether there is an opportunity to develop a product process to organize work activity tasks. On larger, more complex projects, the project manager might be overseeing lower-level managers in charge of work activities who might not have an immediate hands-on supervisory role. That doesn't mean that the project manager can still have an influence over lower-level managers to evaluate work activities for opportunities to develop processes. In some cases, this might be an opportunity the project manager can use to develop a culture of process development with lower-level managers on a project.

The project manager is ultimately responsible for ensuring that all work activities are being completed on schedule and within the budget estimated, producing an output deliverable at a level of quality that meets customer expectations. To ensure that this responsibility has been met, it's in the best interest of the project manager to develop sound processes to manage both the aspects of project management activities and product-related work activities. This chapter focuses on how project management can be a form of process management and how these processes interact with other aspects of a project, as well as areas within an organization.

4.2 Project Management as Process Management

Effective project managers are agents of efficiency through organization and process development and implementation. The very structure of a project includes the development of a project management plan, which in and of itself is an organized development of processes that are carried out throughout the project life cycle. There are many specific tasks that the project manager carries out not only in developing a project management plan but in the course of managing each individual work activity, and these are covered in more detail in Chapter 5, "Project Management Responsibilities." We are looking at a broader scope of management philosophy in which the project manager views the development of a project in the form of processes and how this philosophy drives the organization of a project.

Functional managers know that their department runs more efficiently when they have introduced an element of organization through process development and implementation. This has been the case for decades within organizations because process development has proven itself to be a very effective means of managing work activities. Industries have learned the power of efficiency through process development and have integrated the philosophy of process development throughout all aspects of an organization, including supporting departments such as executive management, accounting, human resources, and procurements. Although these types of departments do not typically have a direct role in producing products and services for customers, they carry out activities on a daily basis that can be organized in the form of processes that streamline efficiency within their respective department.

If we look at project management as a whole, project managers are simply organizing several work activities in a sequential form to produce output deliverables, much like departments throughout a traditional functional organization. If the philosophy of organizing work activities into processes has been successful for most organizations, it would seem reasonable to expect the same outcome in organizing work activities in the form of processes for projects. Just as a functional manager manages departmental processes, so the project manager also simply manages project processes throughout the project life cycle. It is important for project managers to understand how processes are used, what advantages processes give an organization, and how the project manager would use and manage processes on a project.

What Is a Process?

Processes were first developed in the manufacturing sector to organize activities into groups that can be managed more effectively. This can be as simple as organizing a few small steps to carry out one task such as drilling holes in a piece of metal, or as complex as the actions required to prepare a legal document or the steps required to initiate a brand-new product. Regardless of the complexity of activities and what the overall outcome of the steps will produce, it is the effective organization of all actions required to produce a desired outcome, and that is called a *process*.

The Project Management Institute, in its publication of the *PMBOK, Fifth Edition*, defines a project management process this way:

"*A process is a set of interrelated actions and activities performed to create a pre-specified product, service, or result.*"

If functional managers are responsible to ensure that tasks are being completed within their department and have developed the specific steps for each task in the form of processes that are to be performed, the functional manager therefore has the responsibility to oversee processes, not necessarily individual steps within a task. Depending on the complexity of a particular process, a manager might have responsibilities at certain points within the process, but in most cases, individuals identified to carry out processes are trained on the individual steps within a process and are responsible to carry out that process as required on a regular basis. The functional manager actually develops a process to develop processes, train individuals on processes, and monitor and control processes. This is called process management. It should be noted, with regard to project management processes, that we are not talking about the tasks involved in project work activities to create project deliverables, but rather the tasks the project manager conducts in managing all aspects of a project (work performed by the project manager). In the scope of managing a process, the functional manager and a project manager establish six primary areas that define how a project manager develops, implements, and manages a process:

- **Process development**—Processes start out of necessity of a task to be completed and the evaluation of certain steps to complete a task. Tasks can have as little as one or two steps required, or can be very complex, requiring several hundred steps and many details that have to be managed in the course of carrying out the activities steps. Managers should solicit the help of subject matter experts to assist in the development of steps required for a specific task to ensure the task will be completed correctly. As project managers develop processes for work that they will be managing throughout the project life cycle, they can implement a similar process. If the project manager is skilled and knowledgeable about a specific project management task, the project manager can develop the project process for that task. If the project manager does not have the skill, knowledge, or background to develop a process for a specific project management task, it is in his best interest to solicit information from an experienced project manager to ensure that the processes develop correctly.

- **Documenting the process**—After the project manager has outlined the task she will be performing in managing various aspects of the project, it is important to document the process. Documenting a process is important in order to clarify what specific steps are required and in what sequence steps should be performed to ensure that the process is conducted correctly. Documentation is also important in clarifying the details of each specific task. Project managers can then use a documented process as a tool on future projects and can share this tool with other project managers within the organization. It is important for processes to be documented to accurately manage changes that might be required to improve the process if needed.

- **Staffing and training the process**—Much like a functional manager, after developing a process, evaluates each process for proper staffing so the project manager should evaluate project management processes in who will be best suited to carry out a project management process. On smaller projects, project managers are likely to conduct all the project management processes themselves. On larger projects, organizations might have the resources internally to assist project managers in carrying out various aspects of project processes. An example of individuals assigned to assist in conducting project management processes would be resources tasked with cost estimating, schedule estimating, and risk identification. The project manager would then oversee these individuals performing these project management processes.

- **Monitoring and measuring the process**—As processes are carried out throughout the project life cycle by either the project manager or staff assisting the project manager, the project manager is responsible to make sure that processes are performed correctly. The project manager must then develop a system of monitoring and measuring how project management processes are being conducted to ensure that the information required in the communication among staff on the project is accurate and effective in accomplishing project management processes. When project managers will be performing project management processes on their own, they might need to develop a check system to ensure that the processes are being performed as intended. The other important aspect of monitoring and measuring processes is to establish the effectiveness of the process and determine whether improvements are required.

• **Changing the process**—The project manager needs to design a change management system to modify a process if needed. Although processes can be developed and used as tools by project managers, they might determine that minor adjustments need to be made to improve the effectiveness of a process. It is very important for the project manager to evaluate what changes should be made, why they need to be made, and what the expected outcome of the process are if changes are implemented. It is incumbent on the project manager to test a change to ensure that the change accomplishes the intended outcome. If the change seems to have improved the process, the project manager can then update the process document to reflect specific modifications.

• **Evaluation of process effectiveness**—The project manager will want to have visibility of project management processes conducted throughout the project life cycle, whether performed by the project manager or by assisting staff, to ensure that the processes are performing as intended. Because the project manager is ultimately responsible for developing a plan to manage a project, and has developed project management processes to effectively manage a project, the project manager needs to ensure that the outcome of each process is accomplishing the process goal. Project managers must constantly be evaluating each process they develop for constant improvement opportunities because this will be the way the project manager improves not only the effectiveness of managing a project but also the efficiency and utilization of information derived from each project management process.

Project managers are most effective when they view their job in terms of tasks grouped together to form processes. These processes can be documented with all the details required to logically and sequentially perform each task, as well as train staff that might be assisting the project manager to perform project management processes. Project managers are always seeking effective tools and techniques to make their job easier through the organization of tasks that need to be conducted throughout the project life cycle. Project managers also have a tremendous amount of responsibility that can span several aspects of a project that might include interactions with other organizational departments as well as external entities, and the management of these tasks is critical in developing a project.

As we explore the organization project management responsibilities, the first component in evaluating how processes can be developed to manage these responsibilities is to categorize responsibilities into primary groups. These groups can then be broken down into specific tasks that need to be conducted as a function of that group. In some cases, the result or output of tasks conducted in one process group can be the inputs or requirements needed to perform tasks on another process group; these are *process interactions*. This topic is covered later in Chapter 6, "Project Process Interactions." We will first look at how project management responsibilities can be divided into primary process groups.

4.3 PMBOK Process Groups

For the first step in evaluating how processes can be developed for project management, the Project Management Institute has divided project management into five fundamental categories known as process groups:

- Initiating process
- Planning process

- Executing process
- Monitoring and controlling process
- Closing process

Project Management Processes and Interactions

As the project manager evaluates the actions that are typically required to be carried out by the project manager in the course of a project, much like developing any other process, the project must be broken up into fundamental pieces such that each piece can be evaluated for its function within a project. The project manager can focus attention on each individual process group and evaluate the specific actions required for each group. This allows the project manager to develop tools and techniques to manage the tasks within each process group more effectively and efficiently. We will take a brief look at the fundamental characteristic of each process group and some examples of how each group is used on a project.

As we look at project management processes, what these processes are and how they fit within the overall production of a project, these processes are utilized throughout the entire project life cycle, and there must be a clear distinction between the phases of a project life cycle and the project management processes performed throughout the project life cycle. It is easy for students of project management, as well as project managers working in the field, to combine project life cycle phases and project management processes because they do have overlapping components that can be confusing in some cases.

Chapter 1, "Project Structure," explains the details of a project life cycle, and for comparison purposes Figure 4.1 illustrates the phases of a project life cycle. This should be compared to the project management processes shown in Figure 4.2. All projects, regardless of what type of product or service, have basic elements of development that are required to structure a project. Obviously, you cannot start resources on work activities if no work activities have been planned, and likewise you cannot close a project if the project has never been started. There is simply a natural sequence of developmental phases that happen on all projects, and this is called the project life cycle.

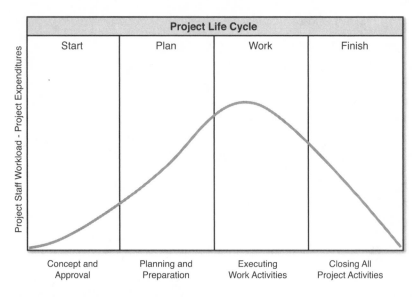

Figure 4.1 Phases of a project life cycle.

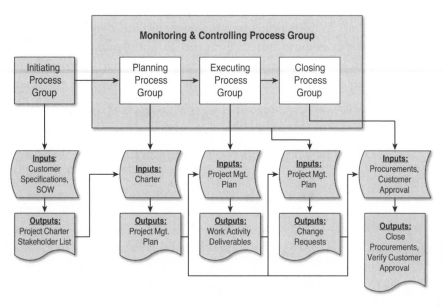

Figure 4.2 Process group and work management.

As we can see in the project life cycle, there are natural stages of evolution a project moves through, beginning with the conceptual phase of understanding the initial scope of a proposed project. The project then moves into a phase of analysis and planning of specific work activities, and then the commencement and management of project work activities, followed by a phase of activities to properly close a project or officially hand off the project to another department. These four elements represent the fundamental components within every project regardless of structure or output deliverable.

When we look at project management processes, we are looking at the actual defined project management processes conducted throughout the project that will have specific input and output requirements. By comparison, the four *phases* of a project life cycle (conceptual idea, planning, project work, and project close) represent the four aspects of a project that inevitably happen regardless of the project structure or deliverable. The term "phase" defines more of a *period of development* through the span of a project. Project management processes are more specific to actual requirements of "work" that must be carried out and responsibilities at each process stage. By definition, a process is a group of tasks arranged sequentially to provide a systematic means to accomplish an objective. Therefore, project management processes are a defined group of tasks to be carried out by the project manager in a systematic form throughout the life of a project. The functions of each project management process are designed to accomplish specific objectives for a project and, depending on the type of project structure, can be implemented throughout the life of a project. An illustration of the five project management processes carried out by a project manager and corresponding interactions of work management is shown in Figure 4.2.

As we can see in the illustration, process groups have a defined function and the project manager has to manage the work required at each process group. Work within each process needs to be managed throughout the project depending on the requirements of a specific project structure. Process group work management is a function of the project structure discussed in Chapter 1. With traditional structures in which a project has a conceptual beginning, a single period for planning activities, a single period to conduct work activities, and a defined closure, the project manager applies the project management processes at each single period throughout the life of the project based on that traditional structure. If the project structure is designed to have several increments or looped processes of planning, work activity, and test, the project manager performs the project management processes several times as needed throughout the life of the project based on the project's structure. Let's examine these five process groups in more detail:

- **Initiating**—All projects start out of necessity, and the necessity can be a very simple requirement of project deliverable all the way to a very large, very complex project deliverable that spans several years to complete. The necessity always starts with a customer requirement and an evaluation of the organization that will be conducting project work activities. Customers can be either internal to the organization or external to the organization. An example of an internal customer requirement might be simply the need within a functional department to create a new process or piece of documentation. Another example might be an organization determining through market surveys that they want to add another product onto their list of products and this new product will need to be developed in their engineering department.

  An example of an external customer requirement is the development of a special product or service that is not typically available in its final form. The customer submits a Request for Quote (RFQ), sometimes referred to as a Request for Proposal (RFP), that includes specifications and descriptions of the project deliverable. An initial evaluation needs to be made as to the feasibility, approximate cost, and time duration required to complete the project objective. All of these actions address the evaluation of a necessity and allow an organization to determine whether a project will be approved. These activities are performed in the *initiating process* phase.

  The initiating process is a critical point for the organization, when the opportunity to provide a product or service is available and a customer has submitted information defining a proposed deliverable. At this point, very little information is known as to all the specific details required to complete the project objective. In most cases, the initial group of individuals tasked with evaluating projects, sometimes referred to as stakeholders, have to use a rough order of magnitude type of estimating to obtain a high-level estimate of cost and time duration for project activities. At this point in the project, there is little or no cost associated with risk assessment, and the organization normally finds itself at a vulnerable point, faced with the decision to approve or reject a project based on this initial information.

In many cases, a project manager is included during this initiating process to formulate high-level project structuring so that work activity costs and durations can be obtained, as well as other information that would help in the project approval process. The primary function of the initiating process is to evaluate information to form an assessment of feasibility for a proposed project and provide a final decision as to a project's approval. The actions carried out during the initiating process can be documented in an initial project document called the *project charter*.

Depending on how an organization is structured to manage projects and how much experience staff has in developing project processes, the project charter can be a literal document outlining all the initiating process proposal information, notes in calculations, and the overall sign-off approving the project. Some organizations that do not have a formal project charter document perform the project charter as a *process in a virtual format* in which all the elements of the charter are conducted and the charter process still takes place, but without a literal document being used. Regardless of whether an actual document is used or the steps within the project charter are conducted as a process within the initiating process, the final output of the initiating process is an approval for the project to take place.

• **Planning**—After the project has been officially approved using the charter process and the initiating process has been completed, the project manager is formally assigned the task of developing a project management plan. Depending on the size and complexity of a project and the structuring of the organization for projects and available resources to assist the project manager through the planning stage, planning a project can be one of the most exhausting periods for the project manager within the development and management of a project.

It is during the planning process that the project manager utilizes many project management skills, tools, and technology to understand the scope of not only the intended deliverable, but also the overall vision of the project and how the project will be structured to accomplish the project objective. A tremendous amount of responsibility is placed on the project manager to properly develop the elements of a project plan. There are several areas in the project plan where the project manager needs to have experience and knowledge of specific project management processes to complete. The Project Management Institute has defined the following areas that need to be planned to form the overall project management plan:

- *Plan integration management*
- *Plan scope management*
- *Plan schedule management*
- *Plan cost management*
- *Plan quality management*
- *Plan human resources management*
- *Plan communications management*
- *Plan risk management*
- *Plan procurements management*
- *Plan stakeholder management*

As we can see, there's a tremendous amount of work included in the planning process, and care should be taken by the project manager and those assisting the project manager to allocate enough time at the beginning of a project for proper planning. The planning process requires the project manager to interact with several departments within an organization and in some cases external information sources.

- **Executing**—After the project manager has completed development of the project plan and a structure of work activities has been established, cost estimates and schedule duration estimates have been completed, and an evaluation of risk has been made, the project manager can then commence work activities. The project manager's responsibility in the execution process is to oversee and manage all work activities to completion, ensuring that the output of each work activity has stayed within the estimated budget, was completed on schedule, and meets the quality expectations established. The project manager uses any and all resources required, as well as tools and techniques to oversee work activities. The scope of responsibility the project manager has over the executing process can vary greatly, depending on the size and complexity of the project. On small projects, the project manager himself can oversee specific work activity tasks, whereas on larger projects in which work activities are vast and complex, the project manager might have work activity managers skilled and experienced in managing specific work activities. The project manager needs to manage all resource schedules and allocations, cash flow requirements, and procurement requirements to ensure that a project activity runs smoothly. Depending on the type of work activities required, the project manager might have several interactions throughout the organization to effectively manage the execution process.

- **Monitoring and Controlling**—The project manager also needs to develop a system or processes that can be implemented to monitor and control work activities on a project. This responsibility is important to ensure that project work activities stay on budget, that they are completed within the estimated time durations, and that the quality of each completed work activity meets quality standards and expectations. The only way the project manager can be assured that these three critical elements are being maintained is to monitor work activities and devise a way to control costs, time durations, and quality to realign work activity tasks to accomplish the activity objective. Designing, developing, and implementing monitoring and control systems can be difficult sometimes, depending on the complexity of each work activity and what is being monitored and controlled. The project manager might solicit information or advice from several departments within the organization as to preexisting monitoring and control systems the organization might have already developed to use on work activities. The information gained from a work activity monitoring system can be used by the project manager not only for control functions but also in the general reporting of activity status.

- **Closing**—The project manager also is responsible to ensure items that have been completed throughout the project are correctly closed. The process of ensuring closure can actually start with the very first work activities conducted on a project and continue until the very last activity is completed. The closing process consists of ensuring that the activity has accomplished its desired output within the specified budget and time frame into the quality expectations that have been communicated. Depending on the type of work activity, some work activities are simple and require only a few tasks and very little equipment, supplies, and materials, and can be closed very easily. Other work activities are very complex and require lots of human resources, equipment, materials, and even facilities that have been obtained for use in the course of the work activity; these require attention to detail to ensure that everything used within a work activity has been returned, everything has been paid for, all contracts have been completed, and deliverables have been verified. These types of situations can present serious financial or legal ramifications if not conducted correctly. It is the responsibility of the project manager to conduct the closing process on every work activity completed throughout the project, not just at the end of the project.

Project Manager's Role in Developing and Managing Processes

The project manager is ultimately responsible for developing just about everything within the project management plan, but there are components to the project manager's role that can be delegated or developed and managed by other resources. Depending on the size of the organization and the type of resources skilled in project management tools and technology, the project manager might be left developing her own tools for project management processes, or might have processes already developed for her use.

Most professional project managers, having skills and experienced in project management, have a propensity for organization and should understand the benefit having well-defined and developed processes. If project managers are employed by an organization that does not have well-defined project management processes, it is typically the role of the project manager to initially establish these processes. If the organization has had prior experience with projects and even has a *project management office (PMO)* in place, standardized templates are used to conduct projects in a systematic and consistent manner. Regardless of the organization's preparedness for project management activities, it always is the responsibility of the project manager to use project management processes to manage activities throughout the life of a project.

- **Project Management Process**—*Development*—The project manager's role is to be educated and trained in project management philosophy, tools, and technology, and to utilize organized and systematic process management processes for the management of all activities within a project. Project managers might be employed by an organization and bring their own knowledge and experience of project management processes with them and can develop specific processes based on the project structures utilized within that organization. Entry-level project managers might simply refer to standardized template processes used in coursework during their education for project management. Some project managers might attend seminars or conventions where they learn better ways to develop project management processes. In some organizations, a project management office is established and the facilitator of the PMO instructs all project managers within the organization as to the processes, tools, and techniques used for project management consistently throughout that specific organization. In this case, the facilitator of the PMO can work as a mentor and trainer to assist project managers in the use of standardized processes.

- **Project Management Process**—*Application*—Because the project management processes are developed for use by the project manager, in most cases, the project managers are the ones using the processes. Depending on the size of the organization and size and complexity of the project, project managers might use project management processes themselves, or on larger projects for which several sublevel managers might be managing several components of a project, the project manager instructs those managers in the application of project management processes. It is ultimately the responsibility of the project manager to ensure that project management processes are carried out, but how this is played out is at the discretion of the project manager. If the project manager chooses to utilize other resources to carry out certain project management processes, the project manager is still responsible to ensure that those processes are being carried out correctly and that pertinent information is being collected and utilized appropriately based on the individual process.

4.4 Project Management Office

As project managers develop and utilize project management processes, they will want to use them on future projects and in many cases communicate these valuable tools to other project managers within the organization. Depending on the size and structure of an organization and how many projects are performed as a typical component of operation, few if any projects might be conducted because an organization simply does not have the requirement for specialized projects, or several projects being conducted simultaneously. If an organization requires a project to be performed only occasionally, they might utilize a functional manager to oversee a specialized project conducted within a specific department. Organizations that utilize projects as a normal part of their operation either contract external project managers or hire professional project managers on staff to oversee projects.

Organizations that utilize projects as part of their normal operation, or are structured to conduct projects as primary components of their operation, require projects to be run efficiently and to stay on schedule and budget, as well as producing output deliverables that meet customer quality expectations. Experienced project managers who understand their responsibility in these types of environments generally have several tools and techniques that they use to conduct a project management processes effectively. Some organizations allow each project manager the flexibility to manage a project the way they choose, whereas other organizations demand that all projects be managed using specific processes for consistency. If specific processes are required in order to manage all projects within an organization, the organization establishes project management templates, tools, and techniques required by all projects. The implementation of this form of project management is called the *project management office*. An organization can structure and manage a PMO in two different forms: *leadership project management environment* and *virtual project management environment*.

The PMO operating under a leadership project management environment is an actual office within the organization, typically managed by a senior project manager or executive to oversee all project management activities within the organization. The project manager in charge of the PMO is responsible for hiring and training project managers. All project managers typically report to the PMO manager directly. The manager overseeing the PMO is responsible for establishing and maintaining project management processes through defined templates, tools, and techniques. The PMO manager's primary responsibility is to ensure that all projects conducted throughout the organization are constructed, documented, managed, controlled, and reported in a consistent manner.

The PMO operating within a virtual project management environment has similar characteristics as the leadership in a project management environment, just without a physical office and manager. The virtual environment takes advantage of ensuring that projects utilize processes tools, templates, and techniques, but store the information on a network environment for project managers to access. Typically one or more project managers within the organization manage the tools on the network and still insist that all project managers use the tools to manage the development, documentation, control, and reporting of all projects within an organization. This type of environment is typical for smaller organizations that do not have a formal physical project management office in place. The PMO basically is used to manage three primary components of project management: *project management platform, project management process templates,* and *project management control.*

Project Management Platform

The first area where the PMO is used is to establish a standardized and consistent form of project management plan development. Depending on the background and experience of project managers, there can be several approaches as to how projects are developed, what is required to define project steps and activities, and how projects are managed and controlled. As we learned in Chapter 1, there can be several types of project structure, and with each type of structure, project managers manage the implementation of project management processes. For instance, if a project manager experienced in overseeing a software development project is used to the structure of software development projects, this type of structure might not be effective if the project manager works for an organization whose primary business is building construction. The PMO is typically developed by project managers with background and experience in projects typical of the organization they are employed by and develop project structure templates appropriate for projects that are used in a particular organization. This is one aspect of controlling project management as new project managers are utilized within an organization.

Some project managers are more familiar with cost or schedule management and might not be familiar with tools and techniques in procurement or risk management, and an established PMO can help project managers utilize existing tools and techniques to ensure that all appropriate project management process areas are developed and managed for projects. Project managers also might share different opinions as to reporting of project activity status, as well as cost and schedule details. This can be frustrating for other management within the organization to receive inconsistent project status reporting from different project managers and can actually foster conflict and confusion based on inconsistent communication techniques. The PMO can be a powerful tool within any organization to create consistency and ensure that projects are developed and managed correctly.

Project Management Process Templates

Project managers work in many types of environments and understand project management structures based on the type of project activities and output deliverables that are produced for projects within their respective organization. In some cases, a smaller organization might employ only one project manager to oversee periodic projects, and that project manager has developed tools and techniques that she uses on every project. Project staff and others within the organization who are associated with her projects have come to understand her particular technique in structuring and managing projects. In this form, she has created her own PMO in which consistency is maintained through the regular use of project tools and techniques. In larger organizations where several project managers are employed, a virtual PMO might be in existence as all project managers have communicated tools and techniques that they all use on each project within that organization and they maintain consistency through their own communication. Typical project management templates include the following:

- Project management plan
- Project charter
- Work breakdown structure (WBS)
- Activity information checklist
- Project scope statement
- Project scope management plan
- Project schedule management plan
- Project cost management plan
- Project quality management plan
- Human resource assessment matrix
- Human resource allocation matrix
- Communication management matrix
- Risk assessment matrix
- Risk register
- Procurement management plan
- Stakeholder management matrix

Project Management Control

The final area in which the PMO comes into play is in providing control over certain aspects of how projects are managed. We know that projects are a function primarily of the organizational structure and how projects are used by an organization. When a PMO is operating within an organization, project managers have guidance on consistent project structuring, planning, and reporting. The PMO functions as a control mechanism to ensure that these three critical areas are maintained for all projects conducted within an organization:

- **Project structures**—Chapter 1 presented several project structuring techniques based on the type of deliverable and project activities required to produce the deliverable. Based on these types of structures, the PMO would play an important role in having an effective structure designed within an organization to manage specific types of projects in all project managers would use those specific structures. Having the PMO control the use of structures would be valuable for project managers as these structures would be fine tuned from lessons learned and prior projects for highest effectiveness and efficiency.

- **Project planning**—Project managers can have a wide variety of experience with various types of projects within different industries and planning for these projects can also have a wide variety of approaches that may vary greatly and effectiveness. The PMO can establish planning tools and techniques to control how project managers plan projects again based on lessons learned and prior projects utilized within an organization. This type of control is important so project managers are planning all the items necessary and will not accidentally miss a critical point of planning due to lack of experience or pressure from time constraints.

- **Project reporting**—One of the biggest complaints from managers, executives, and staff who participate on projects is the inconsistency and reporting of the project status. Project managers have varying opinions as to what needs to be reported and who should receive what types of information. The PMO again serves an important role in providing consistency as to what type of reporting is conducted on all projects. Project status reporting can actually be developed from inputs from other functional managers, executives, and staff or other personnel within the organization who typically receive project status information. A consistent model of project status reporting also takes some of the subjective nature from individual project managers out of the reporting and requires a minimum and consistent level of reporting across all projects.

The PMO—used in either virtual form on a network or actual physical form in an office managed by an upper-level project manager, program manager, or portfolio manager—is a very powerful tool that can be used by an organization to standardize projects for effectiveness and consistency. The PMO is a tool that experienced project managers can have input based on their background and experience that will help build the portfolio of tools and techniques used in the PMO. Likewise, inexperienced or new project managers can utilize very effective and well-developed tools and techniques within the PMO, allowing them to manage projects like the pros. In many cases with small organizations, just a couple of project managers working together can actually start a PMO of their own and utilize their skills and experience, as well as lessons learned on prior projects, to develop more effective project management tools and techniques. It is in the best interest of all organizations, whether functional, projectized, or matrix, to develop a PMO as an organizational strategy to manage projects to ensure that the organization experiences the maximum benefit of the use of projects.

4.5 Summary

Project managers are creatures of organization and find that the most effective plan to managing projects is through the organization of activities called processes. Organizations have found that the organization of activities into processes has made a profound impact on the effective use of resources, as well as efficiency in operations management. The project management world takes the success of processes used throughout industries and utilizes the same philosophy of grouping tasks and activities into project management processes that project managers can use to develop, plan, execute, monitor, control, and close projects.

The Project Management Institute, in their publication of the *PMBOK, Fifth Edition*, identifies five process groups that outline the responsibilities which work activity project managers conduct throughout a project. These five process groups include the following:

- Initiating process
- Planning process
- Execution process
- Monitoring and controlling process
- Closing process

These process groups have critical pieces of work that are performed that either use information from a prior process group or provide information to another process group. The project manager has the ultimate responsibility to ensure that all the work for each process group is completed throughout a project. This is critical to ensure that all aspects of a project are managed correctly. We've also found that information collected within certain process groups can be utilized for another process group, and this forms process interactions.

Project managers must understand how a project impacts an organization and how conducting activities within each process group can affect both the organization and other process groups. Tasks that the project manager performs within a process group can have effects on supporting departments within the organization, such as accounting, procurements, and possibly engineering. These departments might not typically be associated with a particular project, but information from these departments might be required for activities on a project, or information from a project might be used by such supporting departments. Information collected from one process, such as the planning process, are important during other processes, such as the execution process or the monitoring and controlling process. The project manager must be mindful that the accuracy of information collected within each process is important if other processes or departments within the organization rely on this information. It is the ultimate responsibility of the project manager to ensure that all aspects of a project are being managed in such a way that a project can be completed on budget, on schedule, and producing an output deliverable that meets the quality expectations of the organization and the customer.

4.6 Review Exercises

1. Explain how project management processes are used by a project manager.

2. List some of the project management processes within the planning process group, and explain the project manager's role and responsibility in conducting these processes.

3. Explain how project management processes activities in the monitoring and controlling process group can interact with other process groups on a project.

4. Discuss the concept of a PMO, and explain some of the project manager's role in developing, using, and maintaining a PMO.

4.7 Key Terms

Project management process

Project work activity process

Project charter

Product process

Initiating process

Planning process

Executing process

Monitoring and controlling process

Closing process

Process interactions

Project management office (PMO)

Project management control
Project management platform
Project management process templates

4.8 PMBOK Connections, Fifth Edition

1.4.4 Project Management Office

1.5.1 Operations and Project Management

3.0 Project Management Processes

3.1 Common Project Management Process Interactions

3.2 Project Management Process Groups

3.3 Initiating Process Group

3.4 Planning Process Group

3.5 Executing Process Group

3.6 Monitoring and Controlling Process Group

3.7 Closing Process Group

3.8 Project Information

4.9 Case Study

Harmon Decker Medical Center is a large medical office complex that offers a wide variety of medical services, including outpatient medical offices, inpatient medical offices with patient rooms, operating and examination rooms, and emergency room services. This medical complex also has an Advanced Research Center, Psychiatric Center, and Physical Therapy Center. Each of these primary areas within the Harmon Decker Medical Center makes up a division of the overall medical complex. Each division has one or more individual projects running at any given time for special development projects. These projects can range from special research to development of new processes or process improvements, as well as new construction activities.

4.10 Case Study Questions and Exercise

1. Based on the Harmon Decker Medical Center case study, identify areas within each division to use as examples of how projects can be utilized to carry out the completion of specialized objectives.

2. Identify how a PMO could be established and portfolio, program, and project management structures developed to manage project activities carried out in all divisions of the Medical Center.

3. Create an opportunity for a specialized project within one of the divisions of the Harmon Decker Medical Center, and explain what parts of the project would fall into each of the five *PMBOK* process groups.

5

Project Management Responsibilities

5.1 Introduction

The act or process of managing can be interpreted and experienced in several ways depending on the individual's perspective. It's interesting how some individuals might view management as an oppressive function within an organization, whereas others rely on the managers overseeing activities to ensure structure and organization through leadership. It's also interesting how individuals who are not managers can view a management position as being daunting and something that could never be attained, even though in the course of their own responsibilities, they oversee activities and possibly direct other individuals to perform tasks and do not recognize this as some of the basic functions a manager can perform. In the reality of all work being performed within an organization, individuals throughout the organization at all levels organize a component of work or tasks that must be performed and are responsible for some form of output deliverable. This is, in a nutshell, the basic concept of the role of a manager. Another way to look at managing is that everyone in the organization is managing something. It might be a worker simply managing his own time and tasks to complete an objective, a mid-level manager over a product line or workgroup, or a higher-level manager overseeing the entire department or division so that everyone in the organization is managing what they are responsible for.

Individuals with the title "Manager" typically are responsible for the oversight of several tasks and individuals, elevating their position above those that they oversee, and this is why they are called managers. Some organizations have several layers of management, in which executive managers oversee groups of higher-level managers who oversee groups of lower-level managers and so on. Other organizations might have a relatively flat management structure in which the senior executives have all the managers reporting directly to them. In either case, managers have the responsibility of overseeing individuals carrying out work activities that will accomplish the final objective the managers are responsible for.

Projects, being a grouping of work activities, also require a manager to oversee all resources and work activities to complete a project objective, and that is why the manager is called a project manager. Depending on how organizations are structured, projects can be the primary component of work activity within an organization, can be blended with other work activities, or might not be a part of an organization's daily process at all. We will explore the responsibilities the project manager has in each of these types of structures, and how the project manager's responsibilities vary from the responsibilities of other managers within the organization. This chapter also outlines ten of the primary responsibilities the project manager has on a project and gives a brief explanation of the project manager's role within each type of responsibility. Although project managers have oversight of individuals and work activities much like functional managers, we will explore how project managers have to face other interactions internal and external to the organization that functional managers typically do not have to contend with. In this chapter, project managers will understand the difference in skill set and knowledge between project managers and functional managers, as well as the knowledge of responsibilities that will make them successful in effectively and efficiently managing a project to completion.

5.2 Organizational Responsibilities

Most organizations separate various functions that need to be carried out in daily activities and group them by like activities called departments. Examples of departments can include accounting, human resources, engineering, marketing, sales, manufacturing, inventory or warehousing, and shipping and receiving. Because there are specific activities within each of these groups, each group also requires a manager to ensure that specific activities are being carried out on a regular basis. The manager in an organization typically is responsible for the following:

- Planning the activities
- Staffing the department to perform work activities
- Training the staff
- Scheduling staff to perform work activities
- Monitoring and controlling work activities to ensure that they are done correctly
- Verifying that the final output of work activities has accomplished the goal of the department

The term "organization" is used to indicate any form of company, government agency, educational institution, or nonprofit organization that has a strategic objective, management structure, and staffing to carry out daily work activities. Although organizations typically have a structure of work activities that are carried out on a daily basis, they might or might not have projects associated with daily activities, and therefore the role of a project manager can vary depending on the type of organization. Organizations, based on their strategic objective, tactical plan, and operational structure, can be categorized into three primary organizational structures: *functional, projectized,* and *matrix.*

Depending on the type of organizational structure, there are managers responsible for departments throughout the organization called *functional managers,* and *project managers* responsible for the specific activities of an individual project. Functional managers and project managers both exist within a management reporting structure regardless of organizational structure. Some organizations that utilize *projects* as a major component of their operation group projects into *programs* and might even group programs into larger segments called *portfolios.* Managers overseeing programs and portfolios typically are classified as mid-level and upper-level management based on the size of the organization and size complexity of the program or portfolio. Within a traditional operational structure, managers have a defined responsibility that classifies their managerial level within the organization called a *reporting structure.* Managers typically also have a primary responsibility to oversee *human resources* that carry out work activities, and the number of human resources they oversee can also classify their managerial level within the reporting structure. We will first look at three primary components of reporting structure and the responsibilities the project manager has within each type of structure: *organizational structure, project structure*, and traditional *management structure*.

Reporting Structures

Although much has been written about organizational structure and the functional manager's role and responsibilities, this chapter focuses on the roles and responsibilities of the project manager within various organizational structures. The project manager's role and responsibility can vary greatly depending on the size and structure of a company, as well as the type, size, and complexity of projects being carried out within the organization. Defining the role and responsibility as well as reporting structure for a project manager can introduce more complexity because there are other factors to consider outside of the traditional management structure. Variations for defining the project manager's reporting structure, as well as roles and responsibilities, are generally based on one or more of the following factors:

- Whether the organization is structured for projects or has very little experience or use for projects
- Whether projects used in the organization are maintained as single projects or grouped into programs or portfolios
- How the organization classifies the project manager within the overall management structure

To explore these variations in more detail, we will look at three primary structures used within an organization that can help define the project manager's role, and these include *organizational structure, project structure*, and traditional *management structure*:

- **Organizational Structure**—Functional managers have more of a traditional role within the organization in managing all resources required to conduct work activities specific to their departmental objective. As we know, the organization typically is divided into functional groups called departments to help organize work activities and manage departmental objectives, and functional managers are assigned to each department to oversee these activities. When introducing the idea of managing a project, the organization has options as to how to conduct project activities largely based on what the project is accomplishing and how the various types of project activities fall within the normal daily activities carried out by the organization.

The primary question an organization is confronted with, with regard to conducting projects, is why a project would have to be introduced in the first place. The reason we use the term *organization* is that projects can be used in all types of organizations, including for-profit and nonprofit, as well as government and educational agencies and institutes. Some for-profit companies, such as manufacturing, might use a project for creating a prototype product for a customer that will be evaluated for regular manufacturing. Creating one prototype product might be a small part of the overall operation, but it has its place and purpose in managing the evaluation of a new product for manufacturing. Another example might be a construction company that creates large buildings or highway infrastructure in which a large percentage of the operation is managed through projects. In other cases, such as a government agency, projects are not typically a part of the operation, but might be used to manage the modification or creation of a new piece of documentation. In each of these scenarios, the organization utilizes projects differently depending on what the project is intended to accomplish. Because there are variations in how an organization uses projects, organizations can then be classified into one of the three primary organizational structures: *functional, projectized,* and *matrix*. Because the basic concepts of these structures were covered in Chapter 2, "Operations Management Processes," in this chapter, we will evaluate and contrast the responsibility of both the *functional manager* and the *project manager* within each of these three organizational structures.

- *Functional organizations*—Functional organizations have the more traditional structure of departments throughout the organization and have functional managers with assigned responsibility over each department. The application of projects in a functional organization is to manage the creation of process improvements or documentation within each department. In this format, the functional manager typically acts as the project manager overseeing the specific activities for each project. From a project management standpoint, the functional organization has both strengths and weaknesses relative to how projects are developed and managed. In most cases, strengths would be that a functional manager acts as the project manager overseeing a specific project within her own department. This is good because the functional manager knows the scope of the department's normal daily work and can allocate resources for special project activities, allowing the project to be efficient. The functional manager typically has more experience and knowledge with specific aspects of their department and can manage project activities, schedule, cost, quality, and risk as being the resident subject matter expert.

  The weakness of this structure is apparent when the organization selects a functional manager to oversee a project either within the department or outside of the department, and that person might or might not have the experience of a project manager in structuring and managing projects. Although they might have experience with specific aspects of their own department or might be knowledgeable about specific items relative to projects activities outside of their department, they might not have the experience of a project manager in developing, managing, and controlling a project, and the project can suffer as a result. If an actual project manager is employed to manage a project, within a traditional functional environment, the project manager typically carries little or no authority and acts more like an activity expediter. An example of the project manager's role within a functional organization is shown in Figure 5.1.

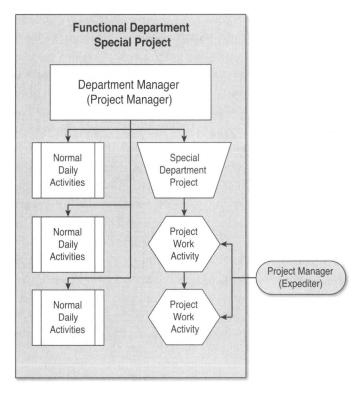

Figure 5.1   Project manager's role, functional organizational structure.

- *Projectized organizations*—Projectized organizations are developed based on the organization having large unique deliverables in which operational activities are grouped and focused on a single output deliverable. An example would be a construction company having the entire staff, or crew, assigned for the creation of a building. The organization might have several crews that each are on an individual, unique project. In this format, the organization has very few if any functional managers, and these large projects are overseen by professional project managers. A big advantage of projectized organizations is the flexibility available in the business strategy. Because this structure emphasizes large projects as its main output, these organizations can respond quickly to changes in market demand, allowing them to be successful in both stable and unstable market environments.

Project management within a projectized organization requires management of activities utilizing different types of resources that can be permanently assigned to the project, borrowed from several departments within the organization, and possibly contracted from resources external to the organization. Unlike a specific project designed to accomplish a goal within a single department, projects are the goal of the entire organization and might require only a few actual departments such as administration and engineering. This type of structure places a high level of importance on project objectives; therefore, project managers are typically hired to structure and oversee projects. The project manager carries a much higher level of authority, with oversight of all resources, budget, and scheduling, and responsibility for completion of the project objective. In most cases, the project manager in this environment holds a mid-level or high-level management position. An example of the project manager's role within a projectized organizational structure is shown in Figure 5.2.

- *Matrix organizations*—Matrix organizations are a blend of functional and projectized structures using the benefits of each in completing the organization's objectives. Matrix organizations typically have a combination of routinely produced deliverables, as well as unique and specialized projects. This allows for traditional departments led by functional managers to manage output deliverables of their individual departments; the organization also is able to use these same departmental resources in special projects. The functional manager still holds authority over her department, but the project manager can hold an equal level of authority in overseeing resources from several departments in managing a project. In the matrix organizational environment, the project manager typically holds a mid-level management position and, depending on the size of the organization, can hold higher-level management positions such as program and portfolio management. An example of the project manager's role within a matrix organizational structure is shown in Figure 5.3.

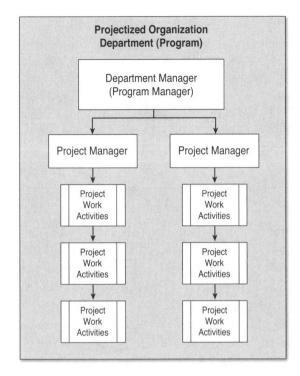

Figure 5.2 Project manager's role, projectized organizational structure.

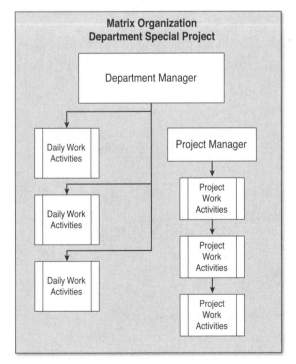

Figure 5.3 Project manager's role, matrix organizational structure.

- **Project Structure**—Organizations that utilize projects to manage activities and objectives can develop a strategy of project management structure in allowing projects to run individually, grouping like projects into elements called programs and grouping programs and projects into larger elements called portfolios. The grouping of projects is largely a function of how the organization is structured, and in most cases organizations structured as *matrix* or *projectized* typically use programs and portfolios. The role and responsibility of the project manager can vary greatly depending on whether he is overseeing a single project or a larger, more complex program or portfolio.

- *Project*—A project is defined as a group of work activities organized to produce a unique, one-time deliverable having an overall time duration defined by a specific start and stop date. The project manager's *role* is to "manage" all resources and work activities to ensure completion and final acceptance by the customer of the project deliverable to accomplish the project objective. The project manager's *responsibility*, in most organizational structures where the project manager has primary authority over the project, is to do the following:

- Develop the overall project plan.

- Develop a work breakdown structure of activities.

- Gather requirements of all resources required for work activities.

- Gather cost estimates of all work activities and develop a project budget.

- Assess activity duration estimates and develop a project schedule.

- Identify potential risks and develop a risk management plan.

- Develop a project activity status reporting plan.

- Create and manage a monitoring and control system for work activities.

- Manage execution of all work activities, including managing budget, schedule, and quality.

- Manage risk responses and contingencies.

- Verify final customer acceptance and approval of project deliverable.

- Close all project activities, procurements, risk contingency actions, and completion of all project documentation.

The listed tasks are generally required for most individual projects and are considered a minimum requirement of responsibility for the project manager in overseeing and managing a project. Depending on the size and structure of the organization, the project manager might have the full responsibility of completing all these tasks or might have other resources available in the organization to assist the project manager in completing some of the tasks. In any case, the project manager has the responsibility to ensure that all the tasks listed have been completed for each project.

As we have seen, individual projects can be conducted and managed by project managers in all three organizational-type structures (functional, projectized, and matrix). The biggest variation in responsibility is in the authority the project manager has over a project, depending on the type of organizational structure. Project managers typically have a much higher level of authority in projectized and matrix organizational structures. In functional organizations, project managers typically see variations in the responsibilities listed previously as to which is performed by the project manager and which is covered by the functional manager or other staff in the organization.

- *Program*—A program is defined as a group of like projects and work activities combined to achieve the program objective. A program might represent a single customer's objective such that several projects are conducted by the organization to satisfy the customer's requirement, forming a *single customer program*. Another example of a program might be several customers interested in a single product, but with slight variations, that constitutes separate projects for development, and this falls under the category of a *single product program*.

The project manager's role and responsibilities on a project, within a program, are the same as a project that is not grouped within a program. The project manager's reporting structure might be different on a project not grouped within a program, because the project manager simply reports to the next level of management as dictated by the organizational structure. Project managers overseeing projects within a program typically report to the program manager. Program managers then report to a higher level of management as dictated by the organizational structure. Figure 5.4 illustrates the reporting structure of both project and program managers within an organization.

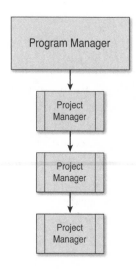

Figure 5.4   Program structure with projects.

- *Portfolio*—A portfolio is defined as a group of programs, projects, and work activities, like or unlike, combined to achieve the portfolio directive. The portfolio manager oversees all program managers as well as any individual project managers within the portfolio. Portfolios are considered to be one of the highest levels of project management structure and portfolio managers are typically senior-level management. In some organizations, portfolios are part of the organizational structure as well as the project management structure and can be considered entire divisions of a company. In other organizations, there might be two or more portfolios inside each division of a company.

The portfolio manager has the ultimate responsibility to oversee all programs, projects, and work activities within the portfolio. Because this is typically a higher-level management role, the responsibility is oversight of program managers who in turn oversee project managers and smaller components of work activity. Figure 5.5 illustrates the reporting structure of project managers, program managers, and the portfolio manager.

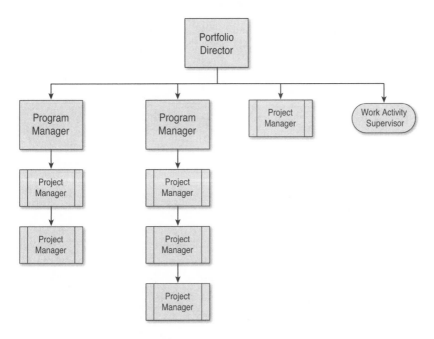

Figure 5.5   Portfolio structure with programs and projects.

• **Management Structure**—All managers working within the organization fall under a management structure of some form. Most organizations have lower-level managers or supervisors overseeing the lowest level of work activity on a product line or small workgroup within a department. Those supervisors and low-level managers report to a mid-level manager such as the department manager, who in turn might report to a high level such as a director or senior-level manager, as shown in Figure 5.6.

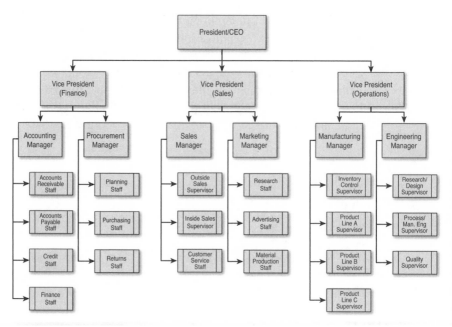

Figure 5.6   Traditional management structure.

Within the traditional management structure, how do project, program, and portfolio managers fall within this structure? Organizations typically organize a management structure, accommodating project management, in one of two ways: either project, program, and portfolio managers are *included in the normal management structure* of the organization, or project, program, and portfolio managers operate within a *special project management structure* that can exist outside of a traditional management structure within an organization.

When organizations maintain project, program, and portfolio managers within the normal management structure of the organization, they are considered to be integrated as one collective body of management. Project, program, and portfolio management roles actually are listed within the management hierarchy as having legitimate levels of authority at low-, medium-, and high- or executive-level management positions.

Some organizations have a special project management structure operating within the management structure of the organization. This project management structure can be referred to as the *project management office (PMO)*. The project management office can be implemented in two forms: operates as an actual physical project management structure, and operates as a virtual project management structure.

The project management office is a philosophy of standardization that can work within a virtual environment in which project managers within the organization utilize standardized project management tools and techniques located on an organization's network. This allows for all projects to be structured the same, and project managers use templates that have been created to standardize project process development and reporting. This allows project managers to follow organized project management standards and maintain consistency for all projects utilized within an organization.

If an organization has an actual physical PMO, this might be managed and operated within an organization that allows the project management structure to exist in hierarchical form independently from the normal functional management structure. The PMO is managed by a director who would also maintain standardized project management templates for process development and reporting, ensuring consistency, and oversees all projects, programs, and even portfolios within an organization. If an actual physical PMO exists within an organization, the director of the PMO is responsible for all managers operating within the PMO and also is responsible for regular performance reviews, salary structures, and promotions.

It is important for project managers to know what type of management structure an organization has because this can play an important part in knowing what level of authority the project manager has and how the organization views that particular managerial role. The project manager needs to know whether the staff on the project are reporting directly to her or are simply being loaned to her for the benefit of the project but still report to their functional manager. Project managers also need to know what level of authority they have with regard to decision making and spending on project activities in order to manage their responsibilities appropriately within their appointed level of authority.

Human Resources

One of the primary responsibilities the project manager has in the overall life cycle of a project is "managing" human resources. As we have already seen, the type of organizational structure can dictate the project manager's role of authority over them and resources assigned to a project. Within functional organizations, projects typically have human resources borrowed from departments to perform specific tasks on a project. These resources still report to their functional manager but simply perform a function on a work activity.

Projectized organizations have operations activities grouped into large projects in which almost all the human resources in the organization are assigned to projects and carry out their daily function on a project until that activity is completed. These resources typically report directly to the project manager until they are reassigned to another project.

Matrix organizations can be a combination or permutation of both functional and projectized structures in which human resources might be borrowed from some departments, whereas other resources might be permanently assigned to a project and report directly to the project manager. Some resources might have only a small specialized task on a single project work activity, and other resources might perform their task multiple times on a project throughout the project life cycle, depending on the type of work activities included throughout the project.

The project manager also has to manage human resources that might not necessarily be directly involved with project work activities, but might have supporting roles throughout the project life cycle, or be human resources contracted externally that are associated with project work activities. These types of resources can be categorized in two primary forms: *internal* and *external* resources:

- **Internal**—Most projects conducted within an organization typically utilize internal human and nonhuman resources for project work activities because this is typically a less expensive and more expedient way to carry out project work activities. Internal human resources can be quickly identified and negotiations with functional departments, if needed, can result in allocations of human resources for project requirements. As we have seen, the organizational structure can play a large part in what types of resources are assigned to a project, whether they are directly responsible for project work activities or resources with supporting roles and not necessarily assigned to a project. The project manager typically manages these two groups of human resources differently, depending on their level of involvement.

  - *Project resources*—These are resources officially assigned to a project and responsible for specific work activities required at some point in the project life cycle. The project manager is responsible for ensuring that these resources have work assignments, monitoring and controlling their work, and verifying the quality of a completed deliverable. Depending on the size and complexity of a project, some work activities might take only a few hours, days, or weeks, whereas other work activities might take several months.

    The project manager must treat human resources assigned to their project as their own employees, whether or not they directly report to the project manager, to ensure that the resource is effective in what they have been assigned. If the resource directly reports to the project manager, the project manager performs the normal managerial oversight activities, such as ensuring that the individual is maintaining the proper attendance and work performance. The project manager can also administer regular performance reviews, pay increases, and possible promotions. If the individual does not directly report to the project manager, the project manager can inform the functional manager to which the resource reports as to their attendance and work performance to provide the functional manager with information to manage that resource.

- *Nonproject resources*—These are human resources not officially assigned to a project or identified as having a specific task within a project work activity. These types of resources still work within the organization, but are in supporting roles such as accounting, HR, quality engineering, facilities and maintenance, and shipping and receiving. The project manager can console would-be supporting departments to gather information or help make a recommendation as to a course of action required on a project work activity. In some cases, the project manager might have to seek permission from a functional manager to discuss a project issue with one of his resources. In other cases, supporting resources have been identified at the beginning of the project as being available if needed. The project manager typically has no authority over these types of resources and generally is at the mercy of the functional manager for the use of her time.

- **External**—Although most projects conducted within an organization try to utilize as many internal resources as possible, it is inevitable that there will be an occasion when an external resource will be required and the project manager will need to understand how to manage these types of resources on his project. External resources are resources not affiliated with the organization and are needed when the organization cannot fill a human resource requirement for a project work activity. External resources typically fall into two primary categories: items that need to be purchased through suppliers or vendors, and human resources that need to be contracted for a specific skill required on a work activity.

  - *Suppliers/vendors*—In most cases, project work activities require the purchase of items such as materials, supplies, tools, equipment, and facilities. If these items are not available within the organization, they need to be purchased externally from a supplier or vendor. The project manager, having organized all the work activities and requirements for each activity, has typically coordinated with the procurements department for purchases that are required. The project manager's role in these purchases is to ensure that the correct items have been purchased at the right time and have been delivered and received undamaged and ready for use. The project manager typically manages obtaining items utilizing purchasing agents to conduct the transactions of these purchases, and shipping and receiving to receive items and verify that they are undamaged. The project manager needs to use tools and establish a system to ensure that purchasing knows what to purchase, at the right time and for a price that the project manager has previously estimated, to ensure that the procurement process is being managed correctly. Depending on the size of the organization, all purchases throughout the project life cycle can be communicated to the purchasing department, and the acquisition of all items required throughout the project can be managed within the procurement department, with little oversight by the project manager. In other cases, the organization might have only limited staff, and the procurement department and the project manager need to take a more hands-on approach in ensuring that all items are being purchased correctly. Regardless of how the procurement department works within a given organization, it is still the responsibility of the project manager to establish a system to ensure that procurements are conducted correctly.

- *Subcontractors*—If a project work activity or task that requires a specific skill in the organization does not have a human resource available to perform this task at the specified time within the project schedule, the project manager must obtain this human resource externally. In most cases, because the requirement of the skill is specific to a particular project work activity, most organizations do not hire an individual as a permanent employee to conduct this one specific task. The project manager solicits a human resource externally for a temporary period to complete the task, and this can be managed under a contract type of employment. This person would be called a *subcontractor*.

Depending on the size and complexity of a project, these specialized skill requirements might or might not be known by the project manager because larger projects might have other resources managing work activities and will have identified specific tasks requiring especially skilled individual. On smaller projects, the project manager might be aware of a requirement and could actually have knowledge of what type of human resource is required to complete the task correctly. In either case, the project manager is required to hire an external human resource to perform the task, and either the project manager or the individual overseeing the task is involved in the interview process to ensure that the individual selected has the skills and experience required.

At this point, an important *warning* should be given to any staff who will be involved in the acquisition of external human resources, by means of a contract agreement, that they need to be well-versed in contract writing and negotiating. The project manager must understand the gravity of the situation and both the financial and the legal obligations of a contract situation. The project manager must also understand that this contract can work in both his favor and his detriment depending on how it is written. Without going into the details of contract negotiation, contracts can be used to clearly define what the subcontractors are required to do, the time frame for the completion of the work, and the compensation for all completed work. Although this seems simple, there can be lots of loopholes written into a contract by the subcontractor that might allow them to be compensated for incomplete or lower-quality work based on a variety of variables in conditions. Contracts can be used successfully by project managers to gain skilled human resources; however, they should be used with caution and only staff within the organization skilled in contract writing in the negotiation should be involved in these types of acquisitions.

5.3 Project Management Responsibilities

Projects come in all shapes, sizes, and complexities, and as we have seen, even the structure of an organization can play an important part not only in the project manager's role and responsibilities but also in how the project manager structures a project. In Chapter 1, "Project Structure," we discovered that there are different types of project structures depending on the type of project deliverable. In this chapter, we are discovering that the organizational structure can also influence not only the authority the project manager has, but also what management responsibilities the project manager carries throughout the project life cycle.

In some cases, the project manager is identified and is a part of the initial team evaluating a project for approval called the charter process. This is usually preferred because the project manager can understand the project from its conception through initial communications with the customer and development of specifications of the project deliverable. In other cases, the project manager is identified after the charter process and project approval and is assigned the development of the project management plan. This is typically less desirable because the project manager then has to review all documentation and generally needs to ask several questions of the evaluation team to understand the specifics of the project deliverable and the overall scope of the project objective. In either case, the project manager is typically assigned the task of developing the overall project management plan.

In many functional organizational structures, the project manager has much less authority, if any, and typically does not have the full responsibility of developing and administering a project management plan. In most cases, functional managers actually develop a project management plan, to the best of their ability, and have the project manager either oversee specific work activities or simply expedite requirements within each work activity to help ensure completion.

In this section of the chapter, we are assuming that the project manager is working within either a projectized or a matrix type of organizational structure and has the primary authority over the project and the responsibility for developing and administering the project management plan. Having the responsibility of developing a master project plan requires the project manager to understand what elements will be required in the project management plan and what the project manager's role will be in managing each area. Depending on the size and complexity of a project, and the size of the organization, project managers on smaller projects typically have to develop the plan themselves with little help by others, whereas in larger organizations and on more complex projects, the project manager might have several staff or even departments to assist in developing major components of the project management plan.

The *Project Management Institute* has solicited the input of thousands of project managers around the world for best practices in developing a project management plan and has consolidated this information into a publication called *A Guide to the Project Management Body of Knowledge*, also referred to as the *PMBOK, Fifth Edition*. The primary responsibilities the project manager has in not only developing a project management plan but also managing project activities throughout the project life cycle have been narrowed by the Project Management Institute into ten categories called knowledge areas. These knowledge areas represent the primary responsibilities of the project manager.

PMBOK Knowledge Areas

Just as projects vary greatly in size and complexity, so does the requirement of what needs to be managed. There are certain aspects of every project, however, that require the project manager to develop a plan as to how they will be managed, reported, and controlled. These aspects are represented in the ten knowledge areas found in the *PMBOK, Fifth Edition*. In some cases, projects might not need all of these items to be managed, depending on the type of project and output deliverable; in other cases, projects might have elements to be managed that are not included in the following list that need to be considered. Because most projects require these ten elements, this is the focus of this section of the chapter.

Note: The opening definition of each of the ten knowledge areas listed is taken directly from the Project Management Institute's *PMBOK, Fifth Edition*, 2013.

- **Integration Management**—*"Project Integration Management includes the processes and activities to identify, define, combine, unify, and coordinate the various processes and project management activities within the Project Management Process Groups."*

The project manager's responsibility, within integration management, is to act as a manager in identifying and managing all processes required in completing work activities. The project manager is also responsible for developing certain processes and tools that are used to assist in managing processes to complete work activities. The project manager is required to develop a monitoring and control system for work activities, as well as a change control management system, to ensure the quality of work activities. Integration management also allows the project manager to identify processes that can be combined, such as managing risk within procurement, or managing communication within human resources. It's important that the project manager understand how various knowledge areas work to form an integrated system of knowledge, leading to action, creating tools that can be used by the project manager.

- **Scope Management**—*"Project Scope Management includes the processes required to ensure that the project includes all the work required, and only the work required, to complete the project successfully."*

  The area of scope management should be taken very seriously by the project manager and project staff, especially at the beginning of a project, when fundamental components of the project are defined. The project manager has the responsibility to gather as much information as possible specific to the project deliverable, to understand the boundaries of the project objective. As the project manager uses this information also to identify specific work activities and formulate a work breakdown structure, it is important for the project manager to stay focused on only what is required to complete the project objective, nothing more and nothing less.

- **Time Management**—*"Project Time Management includes the processes required to manage the timely completion of the project."*

  It is the project manager's responsibility at the beginning of a project, after defining all the specific details of each work activity, to formulate an estimate of the duration required to complete each work activity. These estimates are used in compiling an overall project schedule. The project manager can then use this initial schedule to formulate a baseline to manage and control all project work activities, as well as report the status of the estimated completion of the project.

- **Cost Management**—*"Project Cost Management includes the processes involved in planning, estimating, budgeting, financing, funding, managing, and controlling costs so that the project can be completed within the approved budget."*

As with the project schedule, the project manager is also responsible for developing cost estimates for all requirements within each work activity. The project manager uses these cost estimates to formulate an initial project budget. The initial project budget can be used as a baseline from the beginning of the project, to manage and control all project costs to ensure that work activities stay on budget. The project manager can also use the project budget, throughout the project life cycle, in forecasting cash flow and financing requirements, as well as updates on the budget at completion.

- **Quality Management**—*"Project Quality Management includes the processes and activities of the performing organization that determine quality policies, objectives, and responsibilities so that the project will satisfy the needs for which it was undertaken."*

The project manager is responsible for developing a quality assurance system that includes the monitoring and control of work activities such that the organization's expectation of quality is maintained. Given that quality, time, and cost are typically connected in the development of work activity deliverables, the project manager can use strategies in manipulating time and cost and even resources to ensure that quality is maintained.

- **Human Resource Management**—*"Project Human Resource Management includes the processes that organize, manage, and lead the project team."*

The project manager is responsible for acquiring all human resources required throughout the project life cycle. This can include internal resources with specific task assignments on work activities, the allocation of any required supporting staff not associated with the project but required throughout the project life cycle in a supporting role, and the acquisition of any external subcontracted human resources that are required for work activities. The project manager ultimately has the responsibility to oversee, train (if needed), and "manage" any and all human resources having any connection or association with the project to ensure that project quality is maintained within all project processes. It is also highly recommended that the project manager develop a team environment within the project staff to promote good working relationships, improved communication, and efficiency in completing project work activities.

• **Communication Management**—*"Project Communications Management includes the processes that are required to ensure timely and appropriate planning, collection, creation, distribution, storage, retrieval, management, control, monitoring, and the ultimate disposition of project information."*

The project manager is responsible for developing a comprehensive and effective communication management plan. The development of a good communication plan is critical within project management, because it is the foundation for managing information within the project staff, stakeholders, customers, management, and any external entities such as suppliers and vendors. Effective and efficient communication can be one of the primary tools used to ensure that project work activities are completed on schedule, within the estimated project budget, and meeting the expectations of quality.

• **Risk Management**—*"Project Risk Management includes the processes of conducting risk management planning, identification, analysis, response planning, and controlling risk on a project."*

Dealing with risk management is one of the most difficult responsibilities the project manager has throughout the project life cycle. The project manager's responsibility in managing risk throughout the project life cycle is a formidable component in the success of a project staying on schedule, on budget, and within the quality expectations that are required. The project manager needs to use project management tools not only to identify and assess potential risks, but also to develop a comprehensive response and contingency plan. The project manager also needs to use specific project management tools and techniques to monitor and control work activities to assess early warning signs of potential risk events to mitigate or eliminate any impact to the project schedule, the budget, or the quality of the project output deliverable.

- **Procurement Management**—*"Project Procurement Management includes the processes necessary to purchase or acquire products, services, or results needed from outside the project team."*

  Because most projects have many items that need to be purchased and obtained throughout the project life cycle, this is an area of responsibility the project manager should take very seriously; this is the primary area where problems are imminent. The project manager has the ultimate responsibility in overseeing all procurements, but this does not mean that the project manager has to conduct all procurements. The project manager utilizes project management tools and techniques to effectively communicate procurement requirements throughout the project life cycle, and develop a monitoring and control system to ensure that procurements have been conducted correctly.

- **Stakeholder Management**—*"Project Stakeholder Management includes the processes required to identify the people, groups, or organizations that could impact or be impacted by the project, to analyze stakeholder expectations and their impact on the project, and to develop appropriate management strategies for effectively engaging stakeholders in project decisions and execution."*

  The project manager has the responsibility to develop a system such that the project manager and other project staff can stay in contact with stakeholders to better understand and manage stakeholder needs and expectations. In some cases, stakeholder needs might require only the effective and efficient updating of project status, whereas in other cases, stakeholders might be in a position to offer advice or make decisions and need reliable, accurate, and timely communications to meet their needs.

Stakeholders are an important part of the project team, and it is important that the project manager be sensitive to her responsibilities in association with the project.

These ten areas of project management responsibility form the backbone of the role the project manager plays in developing, managing, controlling, and closing projects. Organizations that employ project managers to oversee projects assume that these basic ten areas of responsibility will be carried out on each project at a minimum. It is for this reason organizations seek project managers skilled and experienced in the tools and techniques of project management to ensure that these areas of responsibility will be carried out correctly. It is the important for the project manager to understand the importance of each of these areas of responsibility because this is what makes project management special within the organization and sets the grouping of project activities apart from normal daily operations. Customers also place high importance on the organization and execution of a project to ensure the timely and effective completion of the project objective. The project manager holds a truly special management position within the organization and is held accountable by their superiors to effectively manage projects that, in many cases, represent business revenue for the organization.

5.4 Summary

Organizations typically have a management structure that is based on the type of organization and how the organization utilizes projects, and this dictates how the project manager falls within the normal management structure. Organizations fall into one of three primary types of organizational structures based on the use of projects: *functional, projectized,* and *matrix.* Project managers employed within a functional organizational structure typically are working on projects within a department, in most cases, overseen by the functional manager of that department. It's not uncommon for the project manager to simply be a project work activity expediter, and reporter of project work status. The functional manager, overseeing projects, can have its strengths and weaknesses, as we have seen, based on the level of expertise the manager has with specific work activities, and the experience the manager has with developing and managing projects. The unfortunate component of functional organizations is the lack of authority the project manager ultimately has in the project, at best holding only a low-level or entry-level management position.

Projectized organizational structures, however, have a complete swing of the pendulum, in which the project manager oversees all aspects of the project and has full authority and responsibility of developing, planning, executing, and closing projects. The projectized structure is used when organizations have projects as their primary business strategy, and thus a much greater importance is placed on the management of projects. The project manager, having a much higher level of responsibility and authority, generally has a higher level of management status within the projectized management structure, usually mid-level to upper-level.

The matrix organizational structure is a hybrid of both the functional and the projectized structures in which the organization is generally divided into functional departments, but projects are common and resources are borrowed from various departments to manage project work activities. The project manager can oversee these projects, having authority over the entire project and the responsibility of developing and executing all work activities to closure. In most cases, the project manager, in the matrix management structure, holds a mid-level management position.

Typically, a large part of the project manager's responsibility throughout the project life cycle is managing human resources. This can be one of the most difficult jobs the project manager will have, because there can be several variables that can challenge the success of using human resources. One variable is the type of organizational structure and the availability of human resources for project work activities. We have seen that the functional organizations work best if a project is managed within a single department and the functional manager can allocate resources based on that department's daily work activities. The projectized structure typically has most of the resources in the organization scheduled for project work activities and, when they are completed on one project, they are simply moved to the next project to utilize their skills. This does present a challenge of resource allocation and scheduling across several projects within the organization. The matrix organizational structure is simply borrowing resources from departments for specific work activities on projects outside of the department, and resources can return to their daily activities after they have completed their project work activity tasks. Managing human resources on projects requires coordinating with functional managers and with other project managers as to effective resource allocation. Project managers also find a challenge in selecting individuals with the correct skill set to effectively and efficiently complete project work activity tasks to make best use of internal resources.

We have also seen a more comprehensive list called knowledge areas compiled by the Project Management Institute in *A Guide to the Project Management Body of Knowledge*, referred to as the *PMBOK, Fifth Edition*, that summarize the core responsibilities of a project manager in what needs to be managed on a project. This list of responsibilities should not be taken lightly by the project manager, because this list was compiled by many project managers around the world as best practices in project management. These responsibilities can also be utilized on small projects as well as very large projects and within all three of the organizational structures covered in this chapter. The Project Management Institute holds project managers to a higher standard of managerial professionalism and ethics because the proper and effective management of projects can mean the ultimate success of an organization.

5.5 Review Exercises

1. Discuss the three primary organizational structures and the basic role the project manager would play within each type of structure, as well as the managerial level the project manager might expect within each structure.

2. Explain the differences in managerial roles given the responsibility of a project, program, and portfolio and what managerial level each would have within the organization.

3. Discuss some of the challenges a project manager might have in managing human resources on a project within a functional organizational structure.

4. List the ten knowledge areas published in the Project Management Institute's *PMBOK, Fifth Edition*—briefly describe the project manager's responsibility for each knowledge area.

5.6 Key Terms

Organizational structure

Traditional management structure

Functional organization

Projectized organization

Matrix organization

Reporting structure

Project management office (PMO)

Internal human resource

External human resource

Project Management Institute

A Guide to the Project Management Body of Knowledge, *or* PMBOK, Fifth Edition

Knowledge areas

5.7 PMBOK Connections, Fifth Edition

3.9 Role of the Knowledge Areas

4.0 Project Integration Management

5.0 Project Scope Management

6.0 Project Time Management

7.0 Project Cost Management

8.0 Project Quality Management

9.0 Project Human Resource Management

10.0 Project Communications Management

11.0 Project Risk Management

12.0 Project Procurement Management

13.0 Project Stakeholder Management

5.8 Case Study

Carmon Events Inc. is a special-events production company that is contracted to design, create, produce, and manage all activities required for large events. These events can be large gatherings such as concerts or speaking engagements, sports events, or special corporate activities events. Carmon Events Inc. has a large facility that houses all of its materials and equipment—sound systems, lighting, tables, and chairs, as well as portable stages and venue materials. Part of the facility is allocated for project administrative support staff, such as accounting, human resources, sales and marketing, and facilities management. The company is divided into three large program divisions: concert events, speaking events, and corporate activity events. Each of these divisions has several projects going at any given time, all led by an individual project manager. Human resources used on projects have special skills that can be utilized on just about any project, and the program and project managers within each division allocate specialized resources depending on project needs.

5.9 Case Study Questions and Exercise

1. Based on the Carmon Events Inc. case study, determine whether this company has a functional, projectized, or matrix organizational structure.

2. Determine whether this company can utilize portfolios, programs, and projects to organize special project activities and resource allocations.

3. Explain the program and project managers' roles, responsibilities, and levels of authority within this company.

6

Project Process Interactions

6.1 Introduction

As we have seen in previous chapters, projects, much like other areas within the organization, are made up of processes carried out to accomplish various objectives. As project managers develop a project and systematically create the sequence of events that will be conducted to complete work activities throughout the project life cycle, the project managers are designing a project as a group of processes, and these processes in many cases have interrelated interactions. The project management processes carried out on a project might have interactions with other projects processes, as well as processes within the daily operation of an organization.

In Chapter 4, "Project Management Processes," project management process groups defined by the Project Management Institute were discussed, but only as single-entity process groups. These process groups include *initiating, planning, executing, monitoring and controlling, and closing.* Each process group, and interrelated activities within each process group, in some cases interacts with other process groups, and these interactions can create various options and outcomes for the project manager. In most cases, many of these process groups have interactions with operations processes, and the project manager must understand not only her responsibility but also how projects can impact the daily operation of an organization. In this chapter, we will discuss in more detail how project management process groups can interact with each other and how these interactions can affect the outcome of a project. We will look at the ten knowledge areas defined by the Project Management Institute and how they apply to projects within process groups. We will also look at the project manager's role in managing various process group interactions and how the project manager can extract valuable information from process interactions that can be used by the project manager as tools for managing a project.

6.2 Basic Project Management Process Interactions

The five project management process groups, as defined by the Project Management Institute in the *PMBOK, Fifth Edition*, reflect five areas of responsibility the project manager has within any type of project structure. The responsibility within each project group is to carry out certain process activities that are required to manage a project to completion. In some cases, interactions can consist of an output of one process group being required as an input to another process group. For instance, the creation of a risk management plan within the planning process group is an output that is used during the monitoring and controlling process as an input for areas of risk management that are to be monitored and controlled. Interactions exist between the project management process groups, but some of the actions carried out in process groups also have interactions with other areas outside of the project in supporting departments within the organization. An example of this interaction is the creation of a procurement management plan within the planning process group that directly affects the purchasing department within the organization. We will look at both interactions of process groups within a project and interactions of project process groups within the organization.

Initiating Process Interactions

The project manager's direct responsibilities within the initiating process group can vary greatly depending on the size of the organization and the size and complexity of a project. In some situations, the project manager might be involved heavily during this process, and in other situations, the project manager is not assigned to the project until the initiating process is complete. If the project manager is directly involved in the initiating process and is responsible for specific actions carried out to complete the project charter process, the initial group of stakeholders including the project manager typically has to interact with several areas of the organization to complete this process. The initiating process group and the closing process group are the two groups with the fewest process group interactions within the project management structure. We will look at interactions within the organization, as well as interactions between process groups:

- **Interactions within the organization can include the following:**
  - *Executive's evaluation* as to whether the project fits within the organization's strategic objective
  - *Executive's evaluation* as to whether the scope of the project is feasible given the organization's level of technology and capabilities
  - *Accounting's evaluation* as to whether funding requirements are available to complete project work activities
  - *Internal subject matter experts' evaluation* of whether critical human resource skill set requirements can be fulfilled with internal staff or need to involve external contracted staff
  - Requirements of the organization's *engineering resources*
  - *Interviews with functional managers* to determine availability of resources required throughout the project life cycle
- **Interactions within process groups can include the following:**
  - Development of the *project charter* within the initiating process is used as inputs in the planning process.
  - Identification of *project stakeholders* in the initiating process is used as inputs in the planning process.

Planning Process Interactions

Although some project managers have experience within certain industries and can derive information without the use of conducting interviews to solicit information, most project managers want updated and accurate information to use throughout the planning process. Based on the level of detail during development of the project charter, and the requirements of project management planning, the project manager likely is soliciting information from almost every department within an organization. The planning process derives several critical pieces of information as inputs from the project charter, and is generating several outputs affecting other process groups within the project.

- **Interactions within the organization can include the following:**
  - *Stakeholder* interviews to further define product scope
  - *Customer* interviews to further define product scope
  - Information required from *engineering* and possibly *production* departments to help define product scope
  - Information from *subject matter experts* within the organization to assist in accurate development of a work breakdown structure
  - Duration estimates might be solicited from *several departments* within the organization
  - Information required from *procurements*, *engineering*, and possibly *production* departments to help define cost estimates
  - *Customer* interviews to define quality expectations
  - Interviews with the internal *quality control* department to define quality expectations
  - Interviews with *functional managers* to identify human resources that are required for project activities
  - Interviews with *stakeholders*, *functional managers*, and others who will be involved in the project for optimum communication methods
  - Interviews with *stakeholders*, *engineering*, *quality control*, and *functional managers* to identify potential risks and obtain information for response strategies
  - Interviews with *procurements*, *accounting*, and possibly *engineering* and *production* to obtain accurate information for critical purchases
  - Interviews with *stakeholders* to understand expectations

- **Interactions within process groups can include the following:**
  - Information from the *project charter* developed in the initiating process is used to develop the project management plan in the planning process.
  - Development of the *scope, cost, schedule, quality, communications,* and *procurement management plans* within the planning process are used within the executing, monitoring, controlling, and closing process groups.
  - Development of the *risk management plan* during the planning process is used in the monitoring and controlling process.
  - Development of the *human resource management plan* during the planning process is used primarily during the executing process.
  - Results of *managing change control* within the monitoring and controlling process is used primarily in the executing process and can be used in some cases in a replanning process.
  - Requirements to *control scope, cost, schedule, quality, communications, risk, procurements, and stakeholder engagement* within the monitoring and controlling process primarily interact with the executing process, but can affect the planning and closing processes.

Execution Process Interactions

The project manager's responsibility of managing all resources, processes, and tasks for the execution process requires the project manager to solicit resources, information, and all things required to ensure that project activities have what is needed to complete each activity. The following are examples of some of the interactions the project manager has within the organization, as well as processes within the project in the course of the execution process:

- **Interactions within the organization can include the following:**

  - Manage the *work breakdown structure* for activity and proper sequencing scheduling.

  - Manage *communication* with departments assisting in the allocation of resources for project activities.

  - Manage *human resource training* and mentoring and the development of the team environment.

  - Manage *conflict resolution* between human resources on project work activities.

  - Manage *cash flow* availability for purchases required for project activities.

  - Manage *procurements* to ensure that purchases are performed in a timely manner such that required deliveries arrive on schedule.

  - Manage *quality assessments* of project activity work to ensure that the output deliverable of each activity meets quality standards.

- **Interactions within process groups can include the following:**

  - Inputs *identifying specific work activities* within the project management plan developed during the planning process are used during the execution process.

  - *Human resources identified* during the planning process to carry out work activities are allocated for those work activities during the execution process.

  - Based on the *communications and procurement plans* developed during the planning process, the project manager implements communications and procurements activities throughout the execution process.

  - *Work activity deliverables* produced throughout the execution process are validated using the monitoring and controlling process.

  - *Work activities completed* during the execution process as an output from the execution process are the input to the closing process.

Monitoring and Controlling Process Interactions

The project manager needs to identify what areas within each work activity need to be monitored and controlled and can determine what type of systems are needed to effectively monitor and control activities within the execution process. The project manager can also solicit the help of departments throughout the organization that can assist in the design, development, and implementation of monitoring and control tools. It is the primary responsibility of the project manager to ensure that work activities are being monitored and controlled to validate work activity cost, schedule, and quality of output deliverables. The following are examples of monitoring and control process interactions within an organization, as well as other project processes:

- **Interactions within the organization can include the following:**
  - Solicit the advice and/or assistance of various departments within the organization as to the *correct methodology for monitoring* a specific element of a work activity.
  - Develop site-specific monitoring tools and techniques for immediate feedback for work activity.
  - *Communicate with departments* such as procurements, quality control, and accounting as to tools that can be in place or information that can be gathered on a daily basis to monitor activities.
  - *Manage external subcontractors'* progress and quality through a monitoring system.
  - Solicit information from various departments such as engineering, quality control, manufacturing engineering, production, and purchasing as to *techniques to redirect activities to control* elements of a work activity that are unacceptable.
- **Interactions within process groups can include the following:**
  - Use *information from the project management plan* developed during the planning process as inputs to develop tools and techniques for the monitoring and controlling process.

- Use *information from the project charter* developed in the initiating process, as well as *information* developed within the planning process as inputs to validate the scope of work activity deliverables during the monitoring and controlling process.

- *Analyze information* from completed work activities during the execution process to control project work activity scope, cost, schedule, quality, risk, procurement, and stakeholder engagement within the monitoring and controlling process.

- *Evaluate change requests* during the execution process using a change management control system within the monitoring and controlling process.

Closing Process Interactions

As the project manager sees each activity come to a close, she is responsible for ensuring that all actions, contracts, and associations connected to the work activity have been terminated correctly. Depending on the size and complexity of a project, the project manager might have several departments within the organization, as well as external subcontractors and companies that play a role in the closing process. The closing process is a critical point for each work activity throughout the project life cycle and is used to ensure that each work activity has been properly terminated and all associations have fulfilled requirements. The following are examples of interactions the project manager has, both internal and external to the organization, as well as other process groups within the project:

- **Interactions within the organization can include the following:**
  - Confirm (with any applicable department) that the desired output deliverable within a work activity has been completed to the expectations set within the activity objective.
  - Confirm with *any department* involved in a given work activity that any items purchased have been delivered and used as intended within a work activity.

- Inquire from the *procurements* department that full payment has been made on purchases within an activity.
- Perform an acceptance audit (within a department if applicable) for an external human resource contracted for work activity to confirm completion of contracted objective and to confirm that all contractual obligations have been met.
- Ensure that all contractual obligations of final payment have been completed.
- Confirm that any rental or leased equipment has been returned and final payment has been made.
- **Interactions within process groups can include the following:**
  - *Evaluate information* within the *project charter* developed during the initiating process, the *project management plan* developed in the planning process, *completed work activities* within the execution process, and *validation of deliverables* within the monitoring and controlling process as inputs to confirm activities required within the closing process.
  - *Evaluate procurements conducted* during the execution process to authorize closure of procurements within the closing process.
  - *Evaluate performance and final acceptance of required deliverables* from *human resources* subcontracted through procurements during the execution process to formally close contracts during the closing process.
  - *Evaluate information obtained for risk management* during the monitoring and controlling process as inputs required for the closing process.

As we have seen, there are many interactions throughout the organization, and even with external sources, that take place in the course of managing the five project management processes. There are also several interactions between process groups in the course of managing project work activities throughout the project life cycle. Project managers must be aware of the impact they can have on an organization in managing these five aspects of the project, and the role the project manager plays in carrying out each of these processes. It is also evident that the project manager requires a significant amount of information and interaction with various departments throughout the organization to effectively carry out each process. It is incumbent on the project manager to understand his role in both developing and managing the five project management processes.

6.3 Knowledge Area Applications

Within each project management process group, certain actions are carried out that not only define the process, but also are critical in the overall completion of a project. The Project Management Institute, in their publication of the *PMBOK, Fifth Edition*, defines ten critical areas of management that interact with various process groups over the course of a project life cycle, and these are called *knowledge areas*. Chapter 5, "Project Management Responsibilities," defines each of the ten project knowledge areas and describes how each is used in the course of a project. In this chapter, we will take the knowledge areas a step further and explore how each of the ten knowledge areas can be connected to project management applications. It is important that the project manager understand the interactions of each knowledge area and how these knowledge areas can support specific applications.

Project Management Knowledge Application

As the project manager develops the project plan and begins to connect the information within each knowledge area to specific process groups, it should become evident that multiple knowledge areas can be used within a process group. The project manager also should understand how various applications, documents, and other processes utilize one or more knowledge areas. Figure 6.1 illustrates how each knowledge area can be utilized and in many cases combined with other knowledge areas to provide input for various project management applications.

| | Applications of Knowledge Areas | | | | | | | | | |
| | Knowledge Areas | | | | | | | | | |
Interactions	Integration Management	Scope Management	Time Management	Cost Management	Quality Management	Human Resources Management	Communication Management	Risk Management	Procurement Management	Stakeholder Management
Project Charter	x	x								x
Project Budget		x		x	x	x	x	x	x	x
Project Schedule			x		x	x	x	x	x	x
Change Control	x	x	x	x	x	x	x	x	x	x
Contingency Plan			x	x	x	x	x	x	x	
Purchase Contracts				x			x		x	
Project Status Updates			x	x		x	x	x		x
Subcontractor Contracts				x		x			x	
Deliverable Test Verification	x	x	x	x			x	x		x

Figure 6.1 Applications of knowledge areas.

Project Manager's Role in Managing Applications

The project manager plays the most critical role in the development of the project management plan, managing each of the project management process groups, as well as the application of knowledge areas within each process group. As we have seen, several knowledge areas can be utilized within process groups and throughout the entire project. It is the project manager's role to manage both the process groups and the application of knowledge areas throughout the project life cycle. The project manager is encouraged to train other staff on the project in the practices of conducting activities within each process group and effective utilization of knowledge areas applicable to each process group.

6.4 Compound Knowledge Area Interactions

The next step in understanding how to utilize project management knowledge areas and process groups is to understand the interactions between knowledge areas and how the combinations and permutations of knowledge areas can produce various pieces of information the project manager can use. In the preceding section of this chapter, we saw how individual knowledge areas and combinations of knowledge areas can be used in applications the project manager needs in various process groups. In this section, we take knowledge area interactions a step further and show how one knowledge area can be used inside of another knowledge area to create information for a project management process forming what's called a *compound knowledge area interaction*.

The basis of a compound interaction is when one or more knowledge areas called *activator knowledge areas* reside or are used within a primary knowledge area called the *function knowledge area*, producing a unique output of information that can be used as a project management tool within a process group. Because one knowledge area alone yields only a certain level of information, one knowledge area can be supercharged with extra information if its output is a function of one or more activator knowledge areas. An example of this compound interaction is shown in Figure 6.2.

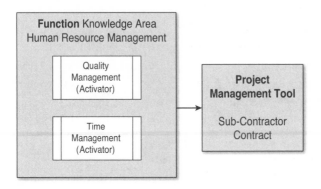

Figure 6.2   Compound knowledge area interactions.

Compound interactions can be used to develop and support project management tools, and as the project manager becomes more familiar with compound interactions, it becomes evident quickly that the information derived from compounding knowledge areas can be used in several applications, as shown in Figure 6.3.

Project managers should always be researching and developing project management processes and discovering how information can be generated, and utilized in the overall development of the project management plan. Project managers should also strive to understand project information in terms of a project management tool and how information can be utilized to accomplish project management processes.

Activator Knowledge Area	Function Knowledge Area	Project Management Tool
Stakeholder Management	Integration Management	Project Charter
Communication Management	Stakeholder Management	Communication Matrix
Quality Management Time Management	Human Resources Management	Subcontractor Contract
Cost Management	Procurement Management	Purchase Contracts
Communication Management	Risk Management	Risk Register
Time Management Cost Management Risk Management	Quality Management	Change Control Process
Stakeholder Management Time Management Cost Management	Risk Management	Contingency Plan
Risk Management	Procurement Management	Subcontractor Contract
Time Management Cost Management Human Resources Management	Scope Management	Work Breakdown Structure (WBS)
Risk Management Time Management	Communications Management	Communications Matrix
Procurement Management Human Resources Management	Time Management	Network Diagram
Procurement Management Risk Management Quality Management	Cost Management	Budget Baseline
Time Management Cost Management Quality Management	Human Resources Management	Resource Assessment Matrix

Left vertical label: Compound Interactions as Project Management Tools

Figure 6.3   Compound interactions as project management tools.

6.5 Summary

We have seen in this chapter how project management is divided into five primary process groups and how these process groups are utilized within a project. Unlike phases that all projects pass through that define particular stages of development, such as conceptual development, planning, work activities, and closure, project management process groups are very specific roles and responsibilities the project manager conducts throughout the project life cycle. Process groups are the primary grouping of activities the project manager conducts in managing the entire project.

As the project manager conducts the activities within each process group, there is certain to be interactions with organizational departments and information the project manager will need to obtain while managing each process group. Unless a project manager has sufficient knowledge, background, and experience with a particular project, and does not need interactions with certain departments, most project managers have extensive interactions with organizational departments. Project managers must be cognizant of the balance between obtaining enough information to manage required activities within each process group, and the intrusive nature the project manager has on various departments within the organization to obtain information.

Project managers can use knowledge areas within process groups to provide inputs, tools, and techniques to manage outputs required within each process group. We have seen that the application of knowledge areas can produce information that can be applied as project management tools. We have also seen that knowledge areas can be combined and through a unique interaction be used to gather in the form of compound interactions to generate valuable information the project integer can use to better define and control project work activities. The project manager must always be aware that the old saying "knowledge is power" is very much the case in project management, and the tools that can be developed by the project manager to utilize knowledge give the project manager more power in the development and control of projects.

6.6 Review Exercises

1. Describe the definition of a project management process and how it is used in project management.
2. Contrast the difference between life cycle phases and project management process groups.
3. Explain the difference between a knowledge area and the project management process.
4. Describe what is meant by a compound interaction.
5. Explain how compound interactions can be used by the project manager.

6.7 Key Terms

Project management processes

Work activity

Production

Process interactions

Initiating process

Planning process

Executing process

Monitoring and controlling process

Closing process

Knowledge area

Compound knowledge area interactions

6.8 PMBOK Connections, Fifth Edition

3.0 Project Management Processes

3.1 Common Project Management Process Interactions

3.2 Project Management Process Groups

3.3 Initiating Process Group

3.4 Planning Process Group

3.5 Executing Process Group

3.6 Monitoring and Controlling Process Group

3.7 Closing Process Group

3.9 Role of the Knowledge Areas

7

Operations Strategy Using Project Management

7.1 Introduction

As organizations grow their operations to accommodate increasing market demand, an important strategy for maintaining successful growth relates to how the operation is organized and managed. Traditional or functional organizations typically place emphasis on a strategy of organizing departments based on specific groupings of work activity. The strategy with a functional organization is to focus on the efficiency of each individual group so that collectively the operation is meeting strategic objectives. As we have learned in earlier chapters, the use of projects within a functional organization is typically limited to the occasional process improvement or development of documentation specific to a particular work group or department.

Organizations utilizing more of a matrix or projectized type of organizational structure have the same emphasis on organizing work activities, but group activities in the form of projects to accomplish both strategic and tactical objectives. Regardless of an organization's structure, operations efficiency can generally be tied to organizing work activities. As more and more organizations discover the benefits of using project management to accomplish both strategic and tactical goals, it is the organizational structure of projects that drives the benefits and efficiency found in project management. Project management can be used by executive-level management to accomplish strategic objectives at higher levels within the organization. In many cases, strategic planning can be vague and has executives looking out into the future to perform long-range planning to better understand primary organizational goals and objectives. Organizations in some cases might utilize project management to accomplish strategic objectives. In most cases, an organization uses project management to accomplish tactical-level goals within the operation. The simple organizational structure of project management and the ease of implementation for smaller scope objectives allow managers to accomplish day-to-day tactical objectives using project management.

Project managers skilled and experienced in overseeing projects discover strategies in managing projects that are complementary to the overall project objective. In many cases, project managers actually manage a project based on a particular characteristic, such as with a cost-prohibitive project, or projects that have significant executive or stakeholder management influence. Project managers can manage projects using strategies to manage high-risk projects and develop tools and techniques that allow them to see future potential risks before they happen. This chapter focuses on several levels of strategy that can be used by both an organization and the project managers in accomplishing operational goals.

7.2 Strategic Use of Project Management

When executives of an organization evaluate future markets and potential directions in which an organization might go, one by-product of this evaluation is the assessment of changes that might need to be made in organizational structures to respond to future anticipated market demands. In some cases, the assessment of the operation might reveal that expansion is necessary, whereas other assessments might deem necessary a change in operational structure, moving from a functional or departmental structure to a more projectized structure. If expansion is planned, executives might use project management to carry out specific expansion objectives such as building new facilities or rearranging equipment within specific portions of the operation to accomplish the strategic goal. If a change in organizational structure is necessary, executives can use project management to carry out activities required to make a change from a functional to a projectized organization, as well as the establishment of specific project management structures required to manage a projectized organization. The benefit in using projects to manage strategic change is the aspect of organizing work activities to manage the components of work individually that will increase the efficiency and effectiveness in completing the project objective.

Manage Organizations' Strategic Objectives

Projects have been used for decades within organizations to accomplish many goals at various levels within the organization. Projects can be used at a tactical level to carry out the simple creation of a document or manage the activities involved in a process development or improvement exercise common in most functional organizational structures. Projects can also be used at the strategic level to manage large changes within the organization. Executives are constantly evaluating areas within the organization for opportunities to expand, change, or terminate particular portions of an operation to best utilize resources for the organization's success. In most cases, changes at the strategic level can be large and require specific project management tools and techniques that allow a change to be conducted efficiently and effectively. Organizations can use projects for several purposes including the following:

- Organize activities to evaluate the overall business value
- Organize activities to expand operations such as the requirement of new facilities
- Organize activities for a reorganization of a particular department
- Organize activities for a special large event held within the organization
- Organize activities for executives to evaluate a specific merger, a new market, or a restructuring exercise

Inasmuch as we have seen the importance of effectively organizing project activities to complete an objective for a customer, the same level of organization and attention to detail should also be used by executives in managing large strategic changes within the organization. In many cases, large changes can be the equivalent of a large project for a customer requiring specifications to be written, a statement of work to be developed, and in some cases, a project charter to be developed and approved by the executive staff. Executives might even employ a project manager to oversee the creation of a project plan to carry out a large strategic change. This would be a wise decision by the executives, because the project manager could also identify a cost structure, develop an overall project schedule, and make a comprehensive risk assessment to manage a large strategic change.

Organize Operations

When organizations evaluate the structure of their operations, it is to assess the overall effectiveness of the utilization of resources to conduct daily operations to meet specific business goals. We have already seen that organizations can be generally structured as functional, with a traditional separation of work activities into departments, or as projectized, in which the organization produces large, unique output deliverables specific to customer needs and organizes the operation to allocate resources to each major project. A third structure is the matrix structure, which typically takes on the form of a functional department but utilizes projects regularly to accomplish tactical goals on a regular basis. Within the projectized and matrix types of organizational structures, in which projects are utilized on a regular basis, organizations can utilize *project management structuring* as a strategic way to organize an operation.

- **Projects, programs, and portfolios**—As we have seen, organizations can utilize projects to manage the completion of tactical goals typically to address customer requirements. We have also seen that projects can be organized into programs as well as portfolios, depending on the size of the organization and how the organization would want to consolidate operations based on product type or customer needs. When an organization has several projects that can be consolidated into programs and further programs and projects consolidated into portfolios, this is actually a strategic-level approach to organizing and operation. We have already learned that the use of these project management structures is typically how an organization manages projects, but now we can see, depending on how programs and portfolios are used, that this is more of a strategic approach to addressing market demands and customer needs.

• **Project management office (PMO)**—When executives within an organization determine that the use of projects, programs, and portfolios is a formidable structure required in daily operations, it is typical to standardize project management processes. This is conducted through the use of a *project management office (PMO)*. The project management office, much like project management structuring, is another way executives in an organization can use strategic planning to manage projects, programs, and portfolios conducted throughout the organization. The PMO is established to control project management structures, tools, and techniques used by project, program, and portfolio managers, as well as a consistent and effective reporting structure.

Manage Customer Interactions

When organizations engage in relationships with customers that represent a large portion of the organization's business, it is important that the organization take these relationships seriously and manage these relationships well. In developing a strategy to manage important customers, it is typically best to develop a process that outlines specific criteria required to effectively manage customer needs, requirements, and communication. Customers, by definition being an entity that has solicited a product or service from the organization, usually evaluate the organization's ability to carry out the customers' requirements. If the organization has a functional structure, projects might not be used very often to manage customer requirements because a functional organization produces similar products on an ongoing basis to meet customer and market demands. If an organization is using a projectized or matrix structure, this would suggest that the customers, on an ongoing basis, have unique product requirements, and each product requirement calls for a project to manage work activities.

Customers requiring specialized products or services need to have an organizational structure such as projects, programs, and portfolios as an operational strategy not only to conduct work activities to meet customer requirements, but also to manage the interactions with the customer. Inasmuch as an organization could probably communicate with a customer as to specific project details without the use of project management structures, the customer's true evaluation of an organization's performance always reverts to what the customer's experience was with an organization. Executives within an organization must understand how the organization manages the customer experience to ensure that the organization is meeting or exceeding customer expectations. The use of project management structures allows the customer to witness an effective organizational tool utilized for the customer's specific needs and optimizes various areas of the relationship with the customer to ensure the best customer experience, which can include the following:

- A single point of contact with the organization is maintained for effectively managing all communication with the customer.
- The project manager is focused on the details of a specific customer product or service.
- The project manager can more effectively manage change control to accommodate customer requests throughout a project life cycle.
- The organization can more effectively manage the relationship with the customer based on the interaction of one project manager versus several staff at various levels within the organization.

The relationship established with customers by an organization is critical to the organization's success, and using projects, programs, and portfolios with a single point of contact is a strategic way executives of the organization can communicate that they appreciate the customers' business.

7.3 Tactical Use of Project Management

Organizations, depending on the size and complexity of the operations, can have various things going on at lower levels of everyday work activity such that projects can be utilized to organize these activities. Organizations might have a structure of operations such as projectized or matrix that utilizes projects on a regular basis as a function of managing operational objectives. Functional organizations that do not typically use projects can also find areas where projects can be utilized to manage activities that might not necessarily be directly related to products or services. It is important for supervisors and managers to understand the benefits that using project management tools and techniques can have at the tactical level within an operation. In some cases, they might already be using tools and techniques and might not be aware that they are actually closely related to fundamental project management tools and techniques. The use of project management tools at the tactical level is categorized into three primary areas: the management of change control, the management of unique work activities, and the management of human resources.

Management of Change Control

All organizations, regardless of the structure, need to change something at some point in time. This might be the change of a document, the product, or a process or procedure. Regardless of what type of change is being made, in most cases changes being made to improve or update something in the success of this update is largely a function of how the change was managed. When you are looking at the requirement of a change, it typically involves several activities that need to be conducted to ensure that important aspects were conducted correctly, and this can best be managed through organizing a change control system in the form of a project. Although a project is simply the organization of work activities to accomplish a specific objective, there is more to project management than just simply organizing activities.

Using project management tools and techniques not only provides a way to systematically organize work activities to accomplish a specific goal, but also allows the following areas of special work activities to be managed:

- Assessment of all costs associated with activities
- Scheduling of all work activities
- Evaluation of potential risks
- Management of all items that might need to be procured for work activities

- Management of quality to ensure that change is conducted correctly

- Development of proper communications with all involved in the project

- Allocation and management of resources to conduct all work activities

- Management of stakeholder needs and involvement

As we can see from the preceding list, there are several aspects of project management that would logically be utilized in managing change control correctly. As we can also see, there is more to project management than just the organization of work activities. Project management tools and techniques are all about the project manager's ability to focus on a specific project objective but to have visibility of the big picture of all aspects of what's required to complete that objective and manage areas of the operation that can influence a project success. A change management process is simply a process developed around the principles of project management to organize all of the steps, processes, resources, and influences required to conduct a change correctly. Examples of how an organization can use project management at a tactical level to manage change within an operation can be seen in process improvements, in product or service evaluations, and in managing the design of experiments.

- **Process improvements**—The first area of change that typically happens within an operation is to conduct process improvement exercises. Process improvements can happen within functional, as well as projectized and matrix, organizational structures. In fact, process improvements and the development of documentation might be the only applications of project management used in a functional organization. Changes to processes or documentation have to be managed very carefully, and using project management to organize the activities involved in an effective and efficient change process can include the following:[1]

---

[1] Wilson, Randal. *The Operations Manager's Toolbox: Using the Best Project Management Techniques to Improve Processes and Maximize Efficiency.* Upper Saddle River, NJ: FT Press, 2013.

- **Propose**
  - *Gather data*—Gathering the data required to evaluate whether a change is necessary can be one of the most important aspects of the change control process. It is vitally important that valid, accurate, reliable, and relevant data has been properly gathered to assess the need for a change.
  - *Develop a business need*—After the appropriate data has been gathered and evaluated, it can be used to develop the details of the scope of the change requested.
  - *Propose change*—After the data has been gathered and a business need has clearly been identified, the change needs to be articulated and presented in the form of a proposal.
  - *Validate and sign-off*—Proposed changes should be evaluated by those who have an interest in or some connection to the process being changed. In some cases, this might be staff who created the original process or it might be those who have influence or oversight of the process. It is important that those selected to sign off on a proposed change not only are qualified to make the assessment that a change is required, but also can validate that a change is successful.

- **Implement**
  - *Conduct changes*—After a change has been approved and signed off on, the activities required to conduct the change can commence.
  - *Manage the scope of change*—When change is being implemented, it's important to note that the change was originally documented with very specific details as to what exactly needs to be changed. The project manager must ensure that activities are conducted within the scope of the original change requirement.
  - *Publicize changes*—When the implementation process is completed, the manager of this change should document that all steps have been completed and the process of this change has been verified.

- **Communicate**
  - *Create a list of those who need to know*—Much as in the beginning of the change process in which a group of individuals were identified as needing to evaluate the change, a list also needs to be generated which communicates that the change has been completed and is now in place. This should include the original group of those who evaluated the change at the beginning of the process, but should also include others such as departmental managers, executive management, or any supporting staff who need to know that the change has been implemented.

- **Measure**
  - *Go back to the original data*—It's the intent of change to make improvements and not to create adverse effects or be a burden on the organization. If data was taken at the beginning of a change which indicated that there needed to be an improvement, the net same data can be taken after the change has been implemented to validate that the change was successful. This should be a requirement within the change process, to validate not only that the change was successful, but also that the investment of resources in the implementation of the change were justified.

  - *Determine whether it is sustainable*—The last part of a change control process is to determine the sustainability of a change after it has been implemented. This type of evaluation assesses the type of change that was made and the integrity of the approach at resolving an issue. Some changes might be simple, as in documentation or policy changes that might simply be reclarifying something or better articulating something that improves the quality of that policy or document. These changes are considered sustainable because they are clarification improvements. Other changes such as organizational structure might initially measure successful, but require time to ensure that the change can maintain success given other organizational influences. In the case of a process and/or product development, these changes can be measured shortly after implementation as to whether they are successful. Process and product changes can be made as needed based on detailed and accurate monitoring that can produce real-time data indicating changes that need to be made. These types of changes need to be measured and verified to validate sustainability.

- **Product or service evaluation**—The second area of change that is most prevalent in organizations is found in modifications made to products or services offered by the organization. Functional organizations that typically provide a service or manufacture products on a regular basis constantly evaluate the product or service to ensure that it is meeting customer expectations. The functional and matrix organizations can employ a project manager and conduct a change control project as listed previously to manage both the evaluation and changes that might be required for products or services. Projectized organizations conduct unique projects based on specific requirements communicated by customers, and the comprehensive change control process listed previously can also be carried out for each change required throughout a project life cycle. The difference in managing the change of a project deliverable is that the change can be based on several factors of customer concern, as well as development of the project deliverable. Reasons for these types of changes might include the following:

  - *Customer requirements of specific form, fit, or function have changed.*

  - *The customer's market condition has forced customer requirements to change.*

  - *Mistakes in the initial specification delivered by the customer need to be addressed later in the project.*

  - *The project manager initiates change to manage work activity quality, cost, or schedule.*

  - *The project manager initiates change to manage supplier quality, cost, or schedule.*

  - *The project manager initiates change to manage potential risks or do damage control.*

- **Management of the design of experiments**—Another example of a tactical use of project management tools and techniques to manage areas within the daily operation of an organization can be in conducting an evaluation that requires a large amount of data gathering and evaluation of data to solve a particular problem, typically within engineering environments or manufacturing environments. This tool is called the *design of experiments*. When a problem has been identified, such as a product performance issue in manufacturing, and initial information suggests several potential root causes, it can be a daunting task to try to figure out which root cause is actually producing the problem. An expensive and time-consuming exercise can be developed to test each root cause through a series of experiments that, depending on the complexity of the product in question, can take several hours if not days or weeks to conduct. If the problem has produced a shutdown in manufacturing, this can have catastrophic effects on an operation, preventing it from being able to produce product.

  An exercise called the design of experiments uses a mathematical matrix of specific pieces of information that produce a statistical assessment of which root cause presents the highest probability of being the actual cause of a problem. This type of experiment is typically carried out in the form of a project in which specific activities have to be well defined and highly controlled to gather specific pieces of information that can solve a specific problem in a fraction of the time it would take to carry out all the tests required to solve a problem. This is an example of using project management tools and techniques at a tactical level to save time, cost, and resources, as well as establish a statistically accurate plan to solve a problem quickly.

Management of Unique Work Activities

Another tactical use of project management can be in the organization of work activities conducted by the operation not associated directly with product production or service provisions. As we have learned, project management is typically used by projectized and matrix organizations to organize work activities that are usually directly related to products or services. Organizations that have departments conducting work activities in support of production and manufacturing, or services being rendered, can also benefit from project management structuring to help organizational workflow, along with new process, product, or documentation development, as well as the organization of large special events conducted by the organization.

- **Primary organizational workflow**—Organizing workflow using project management structures is categorized into two primary areas: organizing the primary work of products or services, or organizing secondary or supporting work. We have already discussed the use of project management structures such as projects, programs, and portfolios to organize work activities resulting in the primary products and services of the organization. We now can look at the tactical use of project management in the secondary or supporting workflows within the organization.

  In structuring both functional and matrix organizations, primary and secondary work activities are grouped into departments. These supporting departments might include accounting, purchasing, manufacturing and process engineering, quality, human resources, warehouse, and inventory control, as well as shipping and receiving. Although each of these departments serve an important role in the overall operations, they typically might not have a direct involvement in producing products or conducting services. Each of these departments, although in a supporting role, has several activities that need to be carried out to support the daily operations of an organization. Managers can use projects to perform the following tasks:

  - *Organize work activities within each department*
  - *Break larger pieces of work into smaller components and outline sequences of events in a work breakdown structure*
  - *Perform a cost analysis of each individual work activity*
  - *Determine time durations of each work activity and develop a schedule*
  - *Plan resource allocations to perform tasks required for each work activity*

- *Perform risk assessments and develop risk management and contingency plans*

  In the same way the project managers use project management tools and techniques to organize project activities and resources, these same tools and techniques can be used in daily operational departments as a tactical way managers can improve the efficiency of their department.

- **New product, process, or documentation development—** Within the organization, processes, products, and documentation need to be developed and maintained, and if they are created from scratch, this gives a perfect opportunity to utilize project management.

  - *Product development*—Because most organizations have a product or service that is offered to customers, occasionally a new product or service might need to be invented or developed. Although a product can be produced on a regular basis, such as within a functional or matrix organization, the initial development of a brand-new product is a one-time and unique endeavor requiring project management. Most organizations, whether functional, matrix, or projectized, use project management at a tactical level to manage the creation of a new product or the development of a new service that would be offered to customers. Using project management to develop products is important to document all the specific steps required to create the product. Project managers can effectively build a cost structure involved in the creation of a project, as well as manage critical timelines in the development of a product based on customer or market needs. Project management also offers the assessment of risks and the development of a risk management plan to ensure that the product is developed on schedule and with minimal influence of risk. Project management can also manage change control during the development of a product to ensure that modifications are validated, implemented, and documented correctly.

  - *Process development*—Because most organizations have processes that are conducted throughout the organization at all levels of work activity, it is common for new processes to be developed on occasion. The creation of a process is also considered a one-time and unique endeavor that can benefit from the use of project management. Much like the creation of a new product, using project management as a tactical tool to manage all the steps required to effectively create a new process is the most effective way to ensure that a process is developed correctly and in a timely manner. The use of project management tools and techniques can help ensure that all the smallest details of a new process are identified and evaluated correctly to build an effective process. Project managers can oversee each stage of the development of a process, which also provides the opportunity for risk assessment and potential problem evaluation.

- *Documentation development*—Much as with the development of a new process, organizations have the requirement to develop documentation. New documentation, depending on the level of sophistication and what the document is actually recording, can range from a very simple project to a very complex project taking a great deal of time and resources. The development of documentation should be conducted using project management. Much like the development of a product or a process, the development of documentation is a one-time and unique endeavor that justifies the use of project management. Documentation can be broken down into subcomponents, and various subject matter experts can be assigned to develop specific parts of a document. The documentation project can have an overall time frame for completion, as well as a statement of work that defines the final output deliverable. Using project management in the development of documentation is again another effective tool used at the tactical level to accomplish objectives within the operation.

- **Special event coordination**—Some organizations, particularly larger organizations, might hold special events periodically that require an enormous amount of planning and resources, and the event itself might be large and complex. Special events can include a company day at a large theme park, a large gathering for a major holiday, or an event to acknowledge something special that requires the organization of several activities. Because this again is an example of a one-time and unique endeavor, project management would be advised to manage all activities of this tactical special event. Project management allows the event coordinator to act as a project manager, outlining all the specific activities that are required to plan and conduct the event. The project manager can also perform a cost analysis of each activity, as well as a schedule duration and risk assessment. The project manager can also formulate a communications plan and a plan for any procurements, as well as contracts that need to be managed in the course of the event. The event has a defined start and end, and it requires a project closeout process to ensure that everything conducted within the event has been properly closed. Project management, although a simple philosophy, can be used throughout the organization for many aspects, to plan, execute, monitor, control, and close work activities. Project management in its complexity is really a simplistic organizational tool that can be utilized for the smallest projects at tactical levels within the operation, on to some of the largest and most complex projects in either tactical or strategic levels within the organization.

Management of Human Resources

The third area in which project managers will use project management tools at a tactical level is the acquisition and management of human resources that will be used on project work activities. In almost every case of projects being used to manage work activities to accomplish a project objective, human resources will need to be used in some way, shape, or form. The fact that an organization has selected a project manager to oversee work activities is the first sign that projects need human resources. Although project work activities could be performed using the elaborate software programs or in the use of automation to perform work activities, projects will need human resources to either manage or carry out the tasks required to complete project work activities.

After the project manager has broken work activities into their smallest components and defined specific work activity requirements, the project manager can identify human resources required to complete certain tasks. In some cases, tasks might require skills and knowledge that are more simplistic and readily available within the organization. Other tasks might be more difficult and require specialized skills, knowledge, or experience critical to the success of an activity. The organization might have human resources with the skills, but if they are not available internal to the organization, the project manager will have to acquire the specialized human resources from outside the organization.

When the project manager plans the use of human resources for project work activities, she will be concerned with four primary areas of human resource management: acquiring project staff, scheduling project staff, assessing work performance, and managing conflict resolution amongst project staff.

- **Acquire project staff**—Project managers evaluate human resource requirements for each work activity in reference to the involvement of specific tasks required. Work activities have human resources directly involved with tasks required to complete a work activity objective. Work activities also have human resources indirectly involved, working in more of a supportive role. Human resources that are directly involved with tasks on project work activities can be defined at two levels: general project working staff and specialized staff.

  - *Direct general staff* is staff that has specific assignments or tasks required to complete a work activity. As a project deliverable will be broken down into it smallest components, this will typically result in a definition of specific work or tasks that will be required and corresponding human resources that will need to be assigned to complete each component of work. This type of work is considered "general," as it may be a common level of work normally conducted within the organization. Resources are readily available within the organization to complete this level of work.

- *Direct specialized staff* is staff that has special skills, knowledge, or experience that would be required for a specific component of work activity. A particular task that might be more difficult than usual or require a much higher level of skill or experience is set apart from the other activity tasks. This special task will require a special human resource assignment. In some cases, the organization might have an individual that will be capable of performing the requirements of the specialized task. In other cases, the project manager might not have to go outside of the organization to hire a human resource with the specialized skill. Examples of this type of specialized skill could be a special engineering function or a level of expertise, such as a craftsman, where the quality of the performance is a key component. The project manager must take care in selecting the specialized individual to ensure that he or she has the skills required to complete the specialized task on schedule and at the quality expected.

- *Indirect project staff* is staff that does not have a direct assignment for specific tasks on project work activities, but performs functions within the organization that support work activities. Examples of supporting staff could include purchasing agents, accounting, executive management, some forms of engineering staff, as well as shipping and receiving. As listed in the preceding examples, these areas within the organization could be utilized on projects but do not necessarily have a specific task that they are assigned that is critical to a work activity.

- **Schedule project staff**—The next critical area project managers are responsible for in the process of managing project staff is in the scheduling of staff for work activities. Most project managers agree that scheduling project staff is one of the hardest parts of planning and managing project work activities. Part of the complexity of scheduling project staff is based on the general organizational structure and whether organizations are structured primarily for projects (projectized), or have more of a traditional (functional) structure of departments and staff reporting to functional managers.

If an organization is structured primarily for projects, this is easier for the project manager, as most staff employed by the organization will work on projects as their primary function. Project managers can simply allocate resources based on necessity, and these human resources move from project to project accordingly. This can present resource scheduling challenges, but in most cases, these types of organizations operate with these conditions as a regular component of their business and they present less of an issue than that of functional organizations. If an organization has a more traditional structure of departments and human resources reporting to functional managers, projects are not utilized very often, and project managers can find it challenging to "borrow" human resources from established departments for project work activities. Project managers can find themselves almost negotiating for the use of human resources and the scheduling of certain resources critical to work activities.

Project managers could also find that human resources have other things in addition to normal work schedules that present challenges for completing work activities, such as other assignments within the organization as well as personal obligations outside of the organization. Human resources also have vacations or sick days that project managers have to take into consideration in scheduling staff to complete work activities. If the project manager has hired specialized staff from outside of the organization, they have to coordinate predetermined work schedules to ensure the outside resources are available during critical times of work activity. The project manager, although developing a strict schedule of human resources required for work activities, must be mindful that these are *human resources* and their availability or reliability may be subject to change without notice.

- **Manage work performance**—Once the project manager has scheduled work activities and human resources required to perform certain tasks, it is also incumbent on him or her to monitor these resources to ensure that they are performing to an expected level of quality and completing tasks in a timely manner. Resources used on projects can perform tasks very quickly, but when work is evaluated, project managers might find a poor quality of work or not all of the requirements of a task complete. On the other hand, resources might be taking so much time ensuring high-quality that the work activities fall behind schedule. The project manager can design forms of monitoring and control that ensure human resources are completing tasks, within the time frame required and at the quality expected.

Project managers that hire staff from outside the organization can manage things such as specific tasks that have to be completed, time frames the tasks have to be completed, and wordage outlining a general level of quality expected through the use of a contract. The project manager can then hold the resource accountable to the conditions outlined in the contract to ensure the tasks are being performed as expected. It is critical project managers pay attention to not only the quantity of work, but the quality of work performed by human resources to avoid rework, insufficient work, or poor quality of work.

- **Manage conflict resolution**—Another important area project managers are tasked with is managing human resources in resolving problems amongst project staff that occur in the course of a project. This is typically one of the most difficult areas for project managers to manage, as conflict resolution requires certain human resource skills and knowledge to be effective. It is advisable that project managers include a representative from an organization's human resource department to assess and aid in conflict resolution. Project managers can then properly document and carry out conflict resolution based on the organization's policies and procedures. If proper policies and procedures are not followed by the project manager, he can cause even more problems for himself and the employees having the conflict, as well as causing potential legal problems for the organization.

As project work activities are completed by human resources, the success of a project can typically point back to the success of individuals completing tasks. Individuals can also be the demise of a project work activity where human resources having conflicts created problems for a project. Project managers must protect their projects from risks stemming from conflict between project staff. In some cases, project work activities might experience only a short delay in schedule to resolve the conflict, whereas in other cases, employee conflicts can result in extended delays and include cost overruns and legal problems that can be devastating for a project and an organization. It is advisable that project managers seek out training for conflict resolution either internally through the organization's human resource department or externally through qualified organizations trained and certified in employee conflict resolution.

Project managers will typically spend a great deal of time planning each work activity required throughout the project lifecycle. Quality time spent in developing a plan to acquire and manage human resources for each work activity is a valuable investment they can make on their project. Human resources are typically critical to the success of a project, so choosing the right resources and managing their time and performance is also critical to the success of a project. Project managers can select the best human resources to work on their project, but if they are not managed correctly the project can still be unsuccessful. Project managers must also understand that their project does not operate in a vacuum within an organization and the resources they are using may have to be used elsewhere in other departments or other projects. Project managers effectively managing human resources on projects is one of the key elements foundational to project success

7.4 Strategies in Managing Projects

Just as we have been looking at both the strategic and the tactical levels of an organization and how project management can be utilized to organize activities, there are also strategies that can be used at the micro level, within projects, to optimize the efficiency and effectiveness of managing a project. Project managers, in having the role of managing project resources to effectively conduct work activities to manage the completion of a project objective, can use certain strategies within a project to accomplish this task. Although the project manager has the responsibility of developing a project plan and implementing this plan through the life span of a project, there can be variations as to how the project manager actually manages work activities.

Projects take on a personality. Whereas some projects are easy to manage, with relatively low-risk activities and human resources that are skilled and experienced in the tasks for each work activity, other projects are very complex and difficult to manage, having a wide variety of experienced human resources, complexities, and potential risks, as well as influences on project costs, schedule, and quality. Some projects are of very short duration, being completed in a few weeks, whereas other projects are stretched out over several months or years. In some cases, projects are conducted in an indoor environment where weather is not a factor, whereas in other cases, projects have to work around seasonal changes that present potential risk.

In designing a project and gathering information for each work activity, as well as assessing the time of year, the location of a project, and all the resources required to conduct work activities, project managers can actually use strategies as to how to best manage a project to completion. Some of these strategies might include the project manager's style and experience, and other strategies might be a factor of the type of project or influences on a project and how the project manager wants to manage certain work activities under particular conditions. Following are some of the more prevalent types of projects and strategies for how project managers can manage projects given certain influential factors.

Proactive Versus Reactive Managing

One of the most influential factors in project success is the management style of the project manager. Individuals selected for project management can be very detail oriented, messy and unorganized, on time to everything, or always late to everything; they can be visionary thinkers, always planning ahead, or the type who is living in the past, always reflecting on "how things used to be." In some cases, executive managers who have employed several project managers might actually take a strategic approach to placing certain project managers over certain types of projects based on their managerial style or personality. Some organizations might simply have to work with the project managers they have in hopes that they can be successful in managing projects. The emphasis here is that executive managers understand the importance of assigning certain project managers to certain types of projects for the highest probability of success.

In most cases, if project managers have experience in successfully leading projects, this is a result of a certain level of organization and attention to detail that is required to manage a project to a successful completion. One primary area in which project managers can differ that can influence the success of a project and determine the general nature of their response to planning, managing cost and schedule, and managing risk is whether a project manager has a *proactive management* style or a *reactive management* style. This can be a very important differentiation based on the type of project. In some cases, this might be more of an important factor during the planning stage, whereas in other cases, this might play a larger role in managing cost or schedule, and in all cases it definitely plays a role in managing risk. Project managers being proactive can actually be a strategic move in managing projects over project managers being reactive. We will look at both of these characteristics of management style and how they play a role as a strategy in managing projects:

- **Proactive**—When project managers are considered to be proactive, the primary characteristic of this trait is the continual compulsion of forward-planning to create road maps based on probable scenarios. As a project manager devises a project plan based on the information gathered, this plan typically represents the most logical sequence of events required to complete a project objective. Because this is the first order of business regardless of any management style, the proactive manager does not stop at simply developing an initial plan; there is an assessment of possible alternative outcomes that drive the proactive project manager to think of other ways in which activities can be done more efficiently. The proactive manager might also assess risks and proactively plan for high-probability risk events in advance to be prepared should they occur. This project manager also plans for scenarios in which procurements might not have been possible based on the original plan and the proactive project manager has backup purchasing ideas that can be initiated without delay of the project.

The proactive project manager is always thinking of better ways project activities can be done, and possible risks that might be on the immediate horizon. When alternative plans can be made in advance, this gives the project manager an advantage because she is already prepared for alternative scenarios to ensure that the project stays on budget, keeps on schedule, and maintains the quality expected in the project objective. The proactive project manager in some cases seems to work with a crystal ball because she is always looking out at the future of the project and thinking of activities before they begin, to ensure that plans are made carefully and backup plans have been developed. The strategy by executive management in using the proactive project manager, if one is available, is to assign this manager to projects that might have critical requirements of cost control, schedule control, or quality control.

- **Reactive**—Most project managers find, in developing a project plan, that a tremendous amount of work is involved in gathering information, developing the project plan, and managing all work activities through to the completion of the project. Most project managers find it successful if they develop a plan and actually finish a project, whether it's on budget or schedule or not. As project managers gain more experience, they can become more efficient in developing project plans and more effective in managing project resources and work activities. When the project manager finds that he is struggling to keep up controlling project costs or the project schedule, there typically is little time to plan for alternatives, and the project manager finds, in most cases, that he feels as though he is simply putting out one fire after another. In many cases, the project manager finds that he is making decisions to solve problems that have already occurred, and this management style is called a reactive response.

  Reactive project managers become very good at solving problems on the fly, having to think out of the box very quickly.

Although this can be a good trade for a project manager, the problem in a reactive response mode is that the project manager is typically under the gun to make decisions and does not have the time to assess the most cost-effective or efficient way to solve a problem. In this scenario, project managers typically default to a more expensive or time-consuming solution that results in success. Some organizations value the reactive response project manager as a valuable asset in being able to solve problems. Although this problem-solving characteristic can be valuable for a project manager, it's only because the project manager has not been able to plan ahead for problems. When project managers are describing their management style, problem solving is an attractive trait for organizations, but proactive planning does not always come across as charismatic management style and might not be understood by some hiring managers.

Being a reactive response project manager does have its benefits when executive management wants to use this strategy for certain projects with a high probability of problems for which the problem solver might be effective. If the reactive project manager can respond quickly and effectively, this can reduce the overall impact that problems can have on a project. Although the proactive project manager might be preferred on many projects, there are certain project types for which the best strategy might be to use a fast, responsive "firefighter" as the reactive project manager.

Steering High-Risk Projects

Because project managers design projects based primarily on an expected output deliverable, there might be occasions when the required work activities throughout the project life cycle have abnormally high risk potential. These types of projects are called high-risk projects, and project managers need to be aware that part of the planning of the project needs to be a comprehensive risk management plan. High-risk projects are addressed here because these are more difficult to plan for and actually require a strategy of risk response to achieve success in managing the project. Most projects typically have challenges in maintaining costs, schedule, and quality, but there are many monitoring and control techniques that can manage these traits on most projects. When projects have the potential for significant impacts due to possible risk events, this requires a special strategy and planning efforts from the project manager. Referring to the project managing traits that we looked at previously, the proactive and reactive response characteristics, a successful strategy in managing high-risk projects is the proactive response manager.

When there is a high probability of risks with significant impact, the project manager must identify these risks early in the project and establish effective response and contingency plans. Proactively planning for each risk, gathering subject matter expert information as to the best course of action for each potential risk, and developing multiple approaches for each risk is how the proactive manager can effectively manage high-risk projects. It is a good trade that the proactive manager also have the firefighter mentality of the reactive response manager to ensure that uncertainties which happen that were not planned for can be addressed quickly and effectively. The primary strategy in the high-risk project is effective for planning of the proactive project manager and comprehensive risk management planning.

Stakeholder-Influenced Projects

Another common characteristic that is difficult to manage throughout a project is the stakeholder-influenced project. This type of project can be referred to as the micromanaged project, because other management, owners, or executive management, and in some cases customers, feel the need to express their own opinions about how a project should be managed, with complete disregard for the project manager. In some cases, the project manager might simply feel like the icon that was assigned to a project name, and others in the organization feel the need to steer the project given their own interests or agendas. The project manager in some cases might have her hands tied, depending on who the stakeholder is and how much power or influence the stakeholder has on the project manager. In functional organizations where projects are typically conducted by functional managers, this can be the case, and there can be confusion as to what the project manager's role actually is. In projectized and matrix organizations, project managers typically hold a higher level of responsibility and authority, and most in the organization afford the project manager the courtesy of managing her own project.

The strategy a project manager should use over stakeholder-influenced projects is for the project manager to understand what type of organizational structure she is working within (functional, projectized, or matrix), as well as understanding what level their direct reporting manager is at and what influence their direct reporting manager could have over other stakeholders. When project managers need to strategize how to manage stakeholders, there are typically two aspects of thought processes that stakeholders might have that drives their compulsion to overthrow a project manager's authority, and these are typically misguided perception and managerial stereotyping.

- **Perception versus data**—One aspect of understanding stakeholders on a project that can include upper or executive management, as well as customers, is how much real and accurate information they have about project activities. In many cases, it is surprising how many executives make decisions concerning projects based on little or no actual data but simple perception of what they think might be happening. People can get second- or third-hand information in an informal conversation in a hallway or break room, or can overhear a sound-bite and misunderstand the context of the information, not having heard the entire conversation. In some cases, information is simply misunderstood, whereas in other cases, stakeholders might have hidden agendas that can drive unwarranted decisions on projects. These types of issues, although common in many organizations, can be unfortunate for the project manager in having to deal with this type of influence, as well as the struggles and stress of day-to-day project work activities.

  The primary strategy used to manage stakeholder influence projects is to first challenge the stakeholder with true data versus their perception. The old saying "it's difficult to argue with data" definitely holds true when dealing with stakeholders making decisions based solely on perception. In most cases, the project manager can understand if the stakeholder in question is operating with little or no accurate data or has an alternative agenda when confronted with real data. If the stakeholder in question is given actual data and was operating off of perception, his influence might be reduced. If the stakeholder in question is operating with an alternative agenda, it does not matter what form of data is presented, and the project manager should realize that the stakeholder is influencing the project for his own personal reasons. The project manager can notify the direct reporting manager or an executive willing to assist in resolving a stakeholder related issue.

- **Managerial stereotyping**—The next primary instance in which stakeholder influence can be seen within an organization is when other managers, executive management, or customers have developed a personal opinion of a particular project manager, called *managerial stereotyping*. If this occurs, it is unfortunate for the project manager because it is difficult to change this type of perception. Typically, there are two ways a project manager can change this reality: by practicing sound project management from the beginning of his career to avoid any undue stereotyping throughout his career, and, if stereotyping does occur on a particular project, by ensuring that the stakeholder in question is included in regular project updates, successful risk events, and information that would suggest that the project manager's performance is clearly not the same as perceived by the stakeholder. Project managers might have run into bad luck on a project and other stakeholders might stereotype the project manager, dooming him for the rest of the life of the project. This can have a devastating effect on both the project manager and the project staff and can actually affect the project's success.

If a project manager has found stereotyping within stakeholders, the project manager should advertise all the successes in the course of managing the project to alter the stakeholder's perception so that he believes that the project manager is performing successfully. The project manager has control over what information stakeholders have and whether stakeholders are operating with simple perception or actual true data of the project manager's performance. It is incumbent on the project manager to ensure that stakeholders receive accurate data so that their perception of a project manager is true and accurate to that data.

Managing Cost-Volatile Projects

Another difficult and common problem lies in projects that have the potential to be plagued by cost volatility. Much like the high-risk project, cost-volatile projects have work activities in which several items have to be purchased or equipment has to be leased or facilities must be purchased that can present challenges for the project manager in controlling costs. Just as most projects involve things that need to be purchased and problems that can arise with purchases, cost-volatile projects have items needing to be purchased that have the potential for the cost to have a wide variance that in some cases might be difficult to control. Again, much as with the high-risk project, part of this problem can be solved through the strategy of planning before the project begins. The project manager, in understanding the details of each work activity, is required to gather cost estimates at the beginning of the project to formulate an overall estimated budget. It is at this point in the gathering of information for work activity costs that the project manager might begin to understand some of the cost volatility that might be present with certain purchases.

The proactive project manager is not happy with simply understanding that there is cost volatility on certain items, but typically wants to gather more information to define the scope of the volatility, as well as the influential factors the project manager could introduce that would reduce the overall spread of pricing. The strategy therefore is in proactive planning and accurate data gathering. In some cases, the proactive manager seeks subject matter expert advice as to the best course of action in managing highly cost-volatile work activities. This is again a strategy of planning at the beginning of the project before these purchases are made, to be ready with actions that can reduce or eliminate such volatility. Further strategies that can be used to manage the cost volatile project include the following:

- **Procurement management**—This is when the project manager takes a direct and proactive approach to communicating certain critical purchases to the procurement department. On the one hand, the project manager might have first learned of the cost volatility from the procurement department, but on the other hand, the procurement department might be completely unaware of the cost volatility if the project manager learned of this through other means. It is the project manager's responsibility to communicate with the procurement department and work with purchasing agents to develop proactive plans to reduce the volatility.

- **Contract management**—Another way the project manager can use strategy in managing cost volatile projects is through the use of contracts. Items can be purchased in several ways, and both parties, the buyer and the seller, typically assume certain risks on most transactions. This is typically due to the uncontrolled nature of undefined aspects of the transaction that can be left for misinterpretation. A contract is simply an agreement between the buyer and the seller to define certain aspects of the transaction that both parties want to record and agree upon. If certain items have a cost-volatile structure, the use of a contract could reduce or eliminate this volatility because the cost structure and other aspects of the transaction can be well defined within a contract. The use of contracts is typically a very successful strategy for project managers, as is using the procurements department in managing volatile costs on a project.

- **Budget at completion (BAC) management**—Another tool the project manager can use in the strategy of managing a cost-volatile project is the use of a *budget at completion* (BAC). Two primary components of the BAC are the overall estimate of project cost and the use of a budget baseline that can be managed throughout the project. One of the primary responsibilities of the project manager at the beginning of a project is to assess all project costs and develop an overall project budget. After the project manager has published the overall budget at completion, the project manager typically assigns either a margin of error or, based on certain volatile components of the project, a plus or minus adjustment window that the BAC can operate within to manage highly volatile projects. It is important for the project manager to communicate to all stakeholders not only the BAC, but also the window of allowance within which the project costs can actually swing, given certain volatile components that might be unknown at the beginning of the project.

The project manager can also use the BAC as a baseline to manage work activity costs on a daily basis. Because the project manager can see what the intended baseline was targeted to be, she can better understand what cost-volatile item is approaching, what the target cost should be, and what the allowable swing in cost is. This gives the project manager information to be in some cases proactive in trying to manage certain costs throughout the project life cycle.

7.5 Summary

Project managers have a tremendous responsibility at the beginning of a project to understand the details of what is required for the project objective, develop a project management plan, and manage project control throughout the project life cycle. In many cases, this seems like a fairly straightforward responsibility, but as we have seen, there can be many factors that can influence a project that require a project manager to use strategy on how to best manage work activities and stakeholders.

Organizations can use projects, programs, and portfolios at a strategic level within the organization to manage resources and customer requirements in daily operations. At a strategic level, executives have several options as to the structure of an organization and how the strategy of project management can be used to complete the organization's strategic objectives. Executives can also use project management at a strategic level to manage customer interactions and relationships.

We have also seen how project management is typically used at a tactical level to manage unique work activities. Organizations can use project management to manage change control within the operations, such as process improvements, special product evaluations, and the carrying out of the design of experiments activities. At the tactical level, project management can be used in functional, projectized, or matrix organizational structures to carry out a wide variety of tactical objectives.

Most important to the project manager, we have seen how strategy can be used even within an individual project. Executives selecting a specific project manager with a particular managerial approach might result in the difference between success or challenge in managing certain types of projects. In understanding the difference between being a proactive response manager and being a reactive response manager, project managers can affect their own success in managing projects. We've also seen how various types of projects, such as high-risk, cost-volatile, and stakeholder-influenced projects, can be managed through the use of certain strategies implemented by the project manager. It is in the best interest of the project manager to always be thinking of tools and techniques as well as strategies for how to manage resources and work activities to effectively and efficiently complete project objectives.

7.6 Review Exercises

1. Discuss what is meant by the strategic use of project management, and give an example of how executives can organize operations with the use of project management.

2. Explain how the use of project management is a strategic approach in managing customer interactions with an organization.

3. Explain what is meant by the tactical use of project management.

4. Discuss some areas of change control at the tactical level where project management can be implemented.

5. Explain what is meant by using strategies within managing projects.

6. Contrast the pros and cons of proactive versus reactive project management.

7. Explain strategies that can be used to manage stakeholder-influenced projects.

7.7 Key Terms

Strategic use of project management

Strategic objectives

Projects

Programs

Portfolios

Project management office (PMO)

Customer interactions

Tactical use of project management

Manage change control

Design of experiments

Strategies in managing projects

Proactive management

Reactive management

7.8 PMBOK Connections, Fifth Edition

1.5 Relationship Between Project Management, Operations Management, and Organizational Strategy

1.5.1 Operations and Project Management

1.5.1.2 Operational Stakeholders in Project Management

1.5.2.2 The Link Between Project Management and Organizational Governance

1.6 Business Value

2.2.2 Project Governance

7.9 Case Study

TC Clarke Aviation is a manufacturer of small fixed-wing aircraft. These semi-custom aircraft are available in either propeller or jet-propulsion systems and can be ordered with customized cabin amenities. TC Clarke aviation has a large manufacturing facility composed of administration and engineering offices, manufacturing buildings, new aircraft storage hangars, and a test airstrip. This aviation company has been contracted by large corporations, wealthy individuals, sports teams, and government agencies to provide custom-outfitted small and medium-size aircraft. The organization designed its own aircraft, manufactures many of their own parts internally, and manages the final assembly of specially designed aircraft.

7.10 Case Study Questions and Exercise

1. Based on the TC Clarke Aviation case study, identify opportunities where project management can be used at the higher strategic level.

2. Discuss several ways in which project management can be utilized at a tactical level within this organization.

3. Discuss opportunities where projects might be used for process improvement, product evaluation, or design of experiments.

4. Give examples of how a project manager might be proactive versus reactive in managing a project within this organization.

5. Discuss examples of how there could be high-risk projects, stakeholder-influenced projects, and cost-volatile projects within this type of organization.

Bibliography

Bender, Michael B. *A Manager's Guide to Project Management: Learn How to Apply Best Practices*. Upper Saddle River, NJ: Pearson Education, Inc. Publishing as FT Press, 2010.

Boone, Louis E., and David L. Kurtz. *Contemporary Business*. Mason, OH: Thompson South-Western, 2005.

Evans, James R., William M. Lindsay, and James R. Evans. *Managing for Quality and Performance Excellence*. Mason, OH: Thomson/South-Western, 2008.

Gido, Jack, and James P. Clements. *Successful Project Management*. 5th ed. Mason, OH: South-Western Cengage Learning, 2012.

Gray, Clifford F., and Erik W. Larson. *Project Management: The Managerial Process*. Boston: McGraw-Hill/Irwin, 2006.

Griffin, Ricky W. *Management*. Boston: Houghton Mifflin, 2005.

Hiegel, James, Roderick James, and Frank Cesario. *Projects, Programs, and Project Teams: Advanced Program Management*. Hoboken, NJ: Wiley Custom Services, 2006.

Jennings, Marianne Moody. *Business: Its Legal, Ethical, and Global Environment*. 9th ed. Mason, OH: Thompson West, 2006.

Kerzner, Harold. *Project Management: A Systems Approach to Planning, Scheduling, and Controlling*. 8th ed. Hoboken, NJ: Wiley, 2003.

Kuehn, Ursula, PMP, EVP. *Integrated Cost and Schedule Control in Project Management*. 2nd ed. Vienna, VA: Management Concepts Inc., 2011.

Morris, Peter W. G., and Jeffrey K. Pinto. *The Wiley Guide to Project Control*. Hoboken, NJ: John Wiley & Sons, Inc., 2007.

Morris, Peter W. G., and Jeffrey K. Pinto. *The Wiley Guide to Project Program & Portfolio Management*. Hoboken, NJ: John Wiley & Sons, Inc., 2007.

Nicholas, John M., and Herman Steyn. *Project Management for Business, Engineering, and Technology: Principles and Practice*. Amsterdam: Elsevier Butterworth Heinemann, 2008.

Pinkerton, William J. *Project Management: Achieving Project Bottom-Line Success*. Hightstown, NJ: The McGraw-Hill Companies, Inc., 2003.

Pinto, Jeffrey K. *Project Management: Achieving Competitive Advantage*. 3rd ed. Upper Saddle River, NJ: Pearson Education Inc., 2013.

Project Management Institute. *A Guide to the Project Management Body of Knowledge* (PMBOK® Guide). 5th ed. Newtown Square, PA: Project Management Institute, 2013.

Vaidyanathan, Ganesh. *Project Management: Process, Technology, and Practice*. Upper Saddle River, NJ: Pearson Education Inc., 2013.

Verma, Vijay K. *Organizing Projects for Success*. Upper Darby, PA: Project Management Institute, 1995.

Wilson, Randal. *A Comprehensive Guide to Project Management Schedule and Cost Control: Methods and Models for Managing the Project Lifecycle*. Upper Saddle River, NJ: Pearson, 2014.

Wilson, Randal. *Mastering Risk and Procurement in Project Management: A Guide to Planning, Controlling, and Resolving Unexpected Problems*. Upper Saddle River, NJ: Pearson, 2015.

Wilson, Randal. *The Operations Manager's Toolbox: Using the Best Project Management Techniques to Improve Processes and Maximize Efficiency*. Upper Saddle River, NJ: FT Press, 2013.

Index

A

acceptance of deliverable, 16
accounting department, project
  interactions with, 101-102
activity information checklist,
  109-110
adaptive project structure, 52-58
Agile
  features addition development,
    47-52
  learn and build development,
    52-58
approval stage. *See* concept and
  approval stage (project life cycle)

B

BAC (budget at completion),
  234-235
benefits of programs and
  portfolios, 118-119
budget
  adaptive project structure, 54
  cost-volatile projects, managing,
    233-235
  extreme project structure, 60
  incremental project structure,
    43-44

iterative project structure, 49
linear project structure, 40
budget at completion (BAC),
  234-235
business conditions, effect on
  project life cycle, 18-20
business operations, projects
  versus, 9-10
business strategy
  strategic level of operations,
    83-85
  tactical level of operations, 85-86

C

case studies
  adaptive project structure, 56-58
  extreme project structure, 62-63
  functional organizational
    structure, 70
  incremental project structure,
    45-47
  iterative project structure, 50-52
  linear project structure, 41-42
  matrix organizational structure,
    73
  projectized organizational
    structure, 71

241